WITHDRAWAL

D1154021

COLD REBELLION

The South's Oligarchy
in Revolt

LEWIS W. JONES

Cold Rebellion

*

THE SOUTH'S OLIGARCHY
IN REVOLT

LONDON
MACGIBBON & KEE
1962

15853

FIRST PUBLISHED 1962 BY MACGIBBON & KEE LTD
© LEWIS W. JONES 1962
PRINTED IN GREAT BRITAIN BY
NORTHUMBERLAND PRESS LIMITED
GATESHEAD ON TYNE

F215
.J74

HARVARD UNIVERSITY
GRADUATE SCHOOL OF EDUCATION
LIBRARY

April 17, 1969

CONTENTS

DEDICATION

TO

Karen, Marion and Andrea

Bare Bones of an Oligarchy

THE 1960 decade began with outbreaks of strife between Negro and white citizens in the southern part of the United States, in what appeared to be also a contest between the federal authority and the authorities of some states and municipalities. The declared intentions of various public officials to 'uphold law and order' called attention to a crazy-quilt legal system that permitted public officials to invoke contradictory laws when statutes suited the convenience and predilections of the adversaries. Interspersed among the news stories of litigation in the courts, police action, controversy and violence there were stories of the celebration of the centennial anniversary of the outbreak of the great rebellion referred to in histories of the United States as 'The Civil War'.

People all over the world would be less puzzled, and many Americans less perplexed, if a simple fact were appreciated by all: the 'United' States have not achieved real unity because federal authority has not undertaken the winning of domestic peace in the ninety-five years since it suppressed the armed rebellion. A cold rebellion has persisted for nearly a century with the Southern rebels participating in the federal government while ruling their domain as an oligarchy—irresponsible to federal authority and contemptuous of federal law.

There should be little surprise that mobs gathered, racial violence broke out, and that there was police indifference to the security of travellers who refused to respect local segregation laws in the South in 1961. That non-segregationists who travelled between states in accordance with federal law should be arrested, judged and jailed for violation of local laws can be made understandable by describing the contradictory political stances of

7

state and federal governments. The State of Alabama under the governorship of John Patterson is a prime example of the travesty of democracy that persists in parts of the American South.

Alabama is a southern one-party state of the United States of America. There the state officials are chosen in 'Primary Elections' in which only members of the Democratic Party vote. The General Elections are merely a formality since no opposition party casts enough ballots to change the decision of the majority party.

In 1958 two Democratic Primaries were held in Alabama. The first one was an elimination in which two front-running candidates were chosen to compete in the second primary. The 'Run-Off' as the second primary is called, gave John Patterson, the successful candidate for the office of Governor of the state, 315,353 votes, a 64,902 majority over his opponent. This was the greatest number of votes ever cast in the state for a candidate for Governor. It was 55 per cent of the total vote cast. It was 32.3 per cent of the potential vote—1,747,750 persons twenty-one years old and over according to the 1950 Census of Population.

Both candidates for the governorship, Patterson and his opponent Circuit Judge George Wallace, were avowed racists but Patterson, as the State Attorney General, had successfully outlawed the National Association for the Advancement of Coloured People in Alabama and had successfully solicited the support of the Ku Klux Klan in his campaign. Following his nomination, the Governor-Designate spoke to a White Citizens Council group saying, '. . . we need more organized groups such as the Citizens Councils.' As Attorney General of the state he had been outspoken in his defiance of the United States Supreme Court. In his campaign for Governor he pledged himself to maintain racial segregation in Alabama regardless of federal court orders to end it.

One of the two Senators from Alabama, John Sparkman, who represents that state in the United States Congress, declared in October 1958 that if a move were made in the United States Senate to outlaw the *filibuster*[1] in the next Congress, 'We

---

[1] A parliamentary device of unlimited debate to keep an issue from being voted on if the majority of the Senators are opposed to the minority of Southern Senators.

(Southern Senators) will meet them at the gate.' In June the same Senator had given an oblique blessing to the violence in Little Rock, Arkansas by saying the mob action in opposition to the desegregation of a high school, 'shows clearly the futility of the federal government trying to legislate people's habits and customs.'

About the peculiar circumstances of political life in the United States there has developed the myth that there is a *mystique* that controls the political order. It is generally believed that customs and habits direct governmental affairs so as to absolve government officials of responsibility for their actions and purposive failures to act which negate the Constitution of the United States, defy the Supreme Court of the nation and challenge the Chief Executive to use his administrative powers. In this volume the mystical rationale is rejected. Men who have political power are held responsible for the conduct of the affairs of the political offices they occupy. The functioning of a political oligarchy is described since it has continued a state of cold rebellion to a last stand position, from which it disturbs the domestic tranquillity of the United States and defaces the proud image of the nation before the world. The task that has baffled and intimidated other Chief Executives of the United States now faces President John F. Kennedy: acceptance of the challenge of the rebels and going about the unpleasant business of ending the cold rebellion by taking away the ill-gotten and ill-used powers of an oligarchy desperate to keep and enjoy them.

Members of the national Congress from the South, Governors, Attorneys General, state legislators, and lesser officials in the South are using every means at their disposal to keep the powers they enjoy. Untruths, half-truths, illogical reasoning, appeals to prejudices, all have generated a dense smoke screen to obscure what they really are determined to preserve. These men have spent untold sums of the tax-payers' money and used hours and days of official time in the defence of their political fortunes.

Notice is taken of the actions and words of noisome southerners because of their positions in state governments in the South or in the national government as representatives of the South. The governors have proclaimed; the legislatures have

A*

passed all kinds of peculiar 'laws' and resolved in several instances to impeach the Supreme Court of the United States;
Attorneys General have given 'legal opinions' and increased
their staffs to fight federal law. Some of these same representatives of government have given strong encouragement to voluntary associations, the White Citizens Councils, which pursue as
a duty States' rights and enforcement of segregation of the
races.

All of these spokesmen for the South beat their breasts in
horror over desecration of the sacred principle of States' rights
whenever federal authority asserts itself to provide safeguards
for citizens denied civil liberties prescribed in the United States
Constitution. They rebuke those who sympathize with desegregation for interfering with racial segregation, which they
insist is a feature of the divine plan made specific in their local
legislation. They make a show of scorn for the ignorance of
those people outside of the South who question their rejection
of the federal authority.

The dominant few claim legitimacy on the basis of the votes
of a small electorate. They consider the affirmation of the
political control they exercise (by a small, almost unanimous,
vote) to satisfy the formalities of democratic procedures. Oligarchs in their loud praise of democracy attribute their control
of power to the accepted values of 'our way of life', 'our democratic system'. They will admit that only a fraction of the
people in the area they dominate can vote or otherwise participate in political decision-making, while they stoutly maintain
that their rule rests on the consent of the governed.

These men seek to make convincing claims that they are
superior, an elite entitled by their exceptional abilities to rule.
Only in a democracy such as this one, they insist, can the able
advance to place and prestige over inherited wealth and social
position. Only under the rules of this 'most perfect' of political
systems can the able be free of the retarding drag of the rabble.
In a debate over rule by an elite, as opposed to mass participation
in government, they will explain that constitutional government
in the United States is really *republican* and not *democratic*, if
you interpret the latter to mean rule by 'the rabble'.

Is it a matter of record that small fractions of the electorate or potential voters cast ballots in the South? Is it not that the smallness of the vote in the elections in southern states is due to the failure of the large Negro populations to qualify themselves to vote? Do not the members of Congress from the South represent overwhelming majorities of the voters in their states and districts? Does it really matter how many or how few people elect them if such able men as Senator Sparkman of Alabama or Senator Fulbright of Arkansas are chosen and serve the nation as capably as these gentlemen have? These and other questions like them are asked when the means of selection of the representatives of these states in the federal government is criticized.

Whatever the answers to these questions posed above are, if the facts and figures support the view that a political oligarchy controls the South and sends its representatives to the national Congress, this group in Congress holds its seats and achieves influence contrary to some fundamental tenets of the political faith of the American people. One of these basic tenets is that in the United States there is representative government. In the words of President Harry S. Truman, 'We believe that all men shall have a voice in their government and government should protect, not usurp, the rights of the people'. A second tenet is like the first one: representatives holding political office are responsive to the popular will. A third tenet is that the two-party system provides an acceptable mechanism for expression of the popular will.

A first inquiry that may easily be made is, how many of the people of voting age make use of the franchise to which they are entitled? How many people actually vote in elections, thereby expressing their consent for government in a positive way? Without the influence of a Presidential election, thirty-four states elected governors in 1954. It is interesting to look at the votes in some of these states and see what proportion of the population of voting age voted for governor. In Republican New Hampshire 194,571 votes were cast in the election. This number was 55 per cent of the population of voting age in the 1950 census. In South Carolina, a Democratic state, 214,204 votes were cast. This number was 19 per cent of the population of voting age in 1950. On the Pacific coast there were 3,908,052 votes cast in the election of California. This number was 54 per cent of the population of voting age. In the governor's election in Texas the vote was 635,654 or 13 per cent of the population of voting age.

We might be curious to know what percentage of the vote cast elected the successful candidate for governor. In New Hampshire, Governor Dwinnell received 55 per cent of the votes cast. In California, Governor Knight received 56 per cent of the votes. Governor Timmerman of South Carolina received all of the votes—100 per cent. Governor Shivers of Texas received 89 per cent of the votes cast.

In Texas and South Carolina where the successful candidates for Governor received 89 and 100 per cent of the votes cast by 13 and 19 per cent of the possible voters, there is obviously government by the few. That is known as rule by oligarchy. In the other states of the South as in these representative two, the percentages of the voting population are strikingly small and the degree of unanimity of the votes cast are unbelievably great.

In the national Congress the 'Southern Bloc' is so entrenched in power and wields such influence that it is considered to be politically dangerous to antagonize its members. Those who have had the temerity to describe it refrain from stating the conclusions that the descriptions warrant. Rule by the oligarchy is shown to rest on a one-party system supported by a narrowly-restricted electorate.[1]

How the one-party system operates is to be seen in the votes cast for twenty-four Senators elected or re-elected to the national Congress from the eleven[2] solid South states from 1956 to 1960. Eleven of those who had no major party opposition received all votes, and of the thirteen who were opposed, nine received more

---

[1] William H. Skaggs, an Alabaman, wrote a little-known book published in 1924: *The Southern Oligarchy, An Appeal in Behalf of the Silent Masses of Our Country Against the Despotic Rule of the Few.* Twenty-five years later *Southern Politics* by Professor V. O. Key, Jr. appeared. Both of these volumes are filled with statistics and facts that describe the governments of the states of the *Solid South* as being oligarchies.

[2] Alabama, Arkansas, Florida, Georgia, Louisiana, Mississippi, North Carolina, South Carolina, Tennessee, Texas, Virginia.

than 70 per cent of the votes cast in the election; in three senate elections in North Carolina in this period each victor received between 60 and 70 per cent of the total vote. The closest election in this period was in Texas where the successful senatorial candidate received only 58 per cent of the votes. The politicians in these states would use these election results to confirm the understanding that they represent the voters in the states where they were elected.

The one-party Democratic states of the South deny that there is any reproach to them in the one-sided vote, and seek to justify it by pointing out that there are consistently Republican states such as Maine and Kansas. The facts are that it is unusual for an opposition candidate in states outside of the South to receive as many as two-thirds of the votes cast. In senatorial elections in Maine in 1958 and in 1960 one successful candidate received 63 per cent and the other 61 per cent of the votes cast. Senatorial elections outside of the South taken at random show the percentages of the votes for the successful candidates to be as follows: Kansas 55, Colorado 52, Idaho 53, Illinois 54, New Hampshire 60 and New Jersey 55. The bothersome statistics show that in Governors' elections in 1954 the Democratic opposition received 45 and 46 per cent of the votes cast in Maine and Kansas.

Southern members of Congress would prefer to ignore the significant fact of the number of voters who elected them and the percentage this number represents of the people who could be expected to vote in their states. The Senators and Congressmen from these states can hardly enjoy being reminded of the percentage of the people in their states that they do not represent, and who had nothing at all to do with their being elected.

Maximum voter participation may be expected in Presidential elections. In the 1952, 1956 and 1960 Presidential elections, 62.7, 65.2 and 63.3 per cent of the population of voting age in the United States as a whole cast ballots. Only one state in the South approached these figures in either election. In seven of the eleven states less than one-third of the potential voters cast ballots. In only one state outside of the South did less than 60 per cent of the population of voting age cast ballots. In many of the states more than 75 per cent of the potential ballots were cast.

When questioned about the limited number of voters in these states, the people who hold offices on the basis of this system grow indignant. They wax vehement in serving notice that the election laws and the political customs of these states are internal concerns, and as such are safeguarded by the sacred principle of States' rights. They will insist that it is a matter of concern only to the people of their states and that they are the voices of the people. These arguments are patently designed to defend a system that gives them power.

The very existence of the oligarchy and the circumstances that produce it is obviously not a matter of concern only to the people it controls. Its influence extends far beyond its direct control. This influence bears on the fate of the nation and on the lives of the people who live in the rest of the United States. In the 87th Congress, as organized in January 1961, chairmen of nine out of sixteen Standing Committees of the Senate were representatives of the Southern oligarchy. Of the twenty Standing Committees of the House of Representatives, eleven chairmen represented the oligarchy. The very rules of the Congress, with their seniority provisions, are hospitable to the accretion of power on the part of the representatives of the oligarchy.

The Congress accepts the representatives of the oligarchy as duly elected members of the Congress, entitled to all the rights and privileges that congressional membership carries. One of the illusions that the Congress cherishes is that only gentlemen and representatives of the American people enter that body. The Congress seems loath to admit that one of its seats has been wrongly come by unless it is contested by an opposing candidate. Given the benefit of the doubt, a member with a dubious voter-mandate may take a non-contested place of influence and power. The American people give sympathetic ear to the spokesmen of the oligarchy and believe in their claims that the South is sorely put upon by misinformed and hostile people outside of the South. These spokesmen take care to establish that they speak for the people, and that their conclusions bring the best and most constructive thought on all issues. The fact that such a spokesman may represent 10 per cent or 25 per cent of the electorate in his state or congressional district might give pause to those who follow his logic.

As a minority in government, these representatives of the Southern oligarchy could not continue to enjoy the power they arrogate to themselves if the Democratic Party outside of the South, the Congress, and American public opinion challenged their claim to representation. The platforms of both major political parties in 1960; action taken by the Federal Civil Rights Commission to ensure the opportunity of Negroes to vote; the Kennedy administration's commitment to safeguard civil liberties with the Executive power—all discomfort the oligarchy. The course of events has brought a spirit of desperation to the oligarchy, which sees its ill-gotten power threatened and its undue privileges taken away.

Unfailingly, members of the oligarchy outshout all others in the defence or advancement of democracy—their version. As a matter of fact they strive to be convincing in their claims that their way is the true version of revealed democratic gospel. They gave it a fresh statement in a *Declaration of Constitutional Principles* in 1956. No one would argue that in a democracy 96 members of Congress should not be heard, or that when they have a common point of view they should not express it jointly. They should have this hearing whether they represent the majority or a minority of the people in the eleven states, merely one-fourth of the nation, from which they come. Having heard them out, it is well to consider for whom they speak and why they speak as they do. Is the statement made a special pleading for their own political fortune? Is it misunderstanding of the South that they resent, or is it too clear an understanding of the South that they fear?

PART I

Power to the Few—
Historical Perspective

Power to the Few—
HISTORICAL PERSPECTIVE

BETWEEN 1890 and 1910 the Southern states rewrote their Constitutions. The pressing need for constitutional reform arose from the universal suffrage provisions in the constitutions adopted by the rebellious states to gain re-admission to the Union, following military defeat of the Confederacy. Those constitutions, as adopted by loyal citizens of the states, denied the vote only to disloyal citizens who had borne arms against the United States. The Fourteenth Amendment to the United States Constitution, declared ratified by the States, July 28, 1868, provided that the vote should be denied only to those who had engaged in rebellion, or had been adjudged guilty of other crimes, and provided for representation in the national Congress on the basis of the proportion which voting male citizens represent of the electorate. The Fifteenth Amendment, which was declared ratified on March 30, 1870 specifically provided:

> The right of the citizens of the United States to vote shall not be denied or abridged by the United States or by any State on account of race, colour or previous condition of servitude.

Those rebellious in spirit proceeded forthwith to negate these constitutional provisions by the use of violence and chicanery.

As the defeated rebels regained *de facto* power, they sought to legalize their control of state and local governments by making for their states new constitutions into which it was written that the franchise belonged to them. Deliberate care was taken over voter qualification clauses which would effectively cull the electorate and create a legal basis for government by oligarchy.

The pretext that made voter restrictions in the new state constitutions acceptable to many was that they were designed to disfranchise Negroes in direct defiance of the Fourteenth and Fifteenth Amendments. The pre-eminent Negro of the time

19

warned against the consequences of voter restriction in appeals
to the Louisiana constitutional convention in 1898 and to the
Alabama convention in 1901. In his letter to the Louisiana convention, Booker T. Washington wrote:

' Since the war, no State has had such an opportunity to settle
for all time the race question, so far as it concerns politics, as
is now given in Louisiana. Will your convention set an
example to the world in this respect? Will Louisiana take such
high and just grounds in respect to the Negro that no one
can doubt that the South is as good a friend to the Negro as
he possesses elsewhere? In all this, gentlemen of the Convention, I am not pleading for the Negro alone, but for the morals,
the higher life of the white man as well. For the more I study
the question, the more I am convinced that it is not so much
a question as to what the white man will do with the
Negro, as to what the Negro will do with the white man's
civilization.

' The Negro agrees with you that it is necessary to the
salvation of the South that restriction be put upon the ballot.
I know that you have two serious problems before you;
ignorant and corrupt government on the one hand, and on
the other hand a way to restrict the ballot so that control will
be in the hands of the intelligent without regard to race. With
the sincerest sympathy with you in your efforts to find a way
out of the difficulty, I want to suggest that no State in the
South can make a law that will provide an opportunity or
temptation for an ignorant white man to vote and withhold
the same opportunity from an ignorant coloured man, without
injuring both men. No State can make a law that can thus be
executed, without dwarfing for all time the morals of the
white man in the South. Any law controlling the ballot, that
is not absolutely just and fair to both races, will work more
permanent injury to the whites than to the blacks.'

Letter from Booker T. Washington to the Louisiana State
Constitutional Convention, February 19, 1898.

A newspaper interview in 1900 in the *Atlanta Constitution*

quoted Dr Washington using words of the President of Yale University to support his views on the Hardwick Bill. This bill was before the Georgia Legislature and sought to control the franchise by use of an 'understanding' clause. Dr Washington is quoted as saying:

'To pass an election law with an "understanding" clause, simply means that some individual will be tempted to perjure his soul and degrade his whole life by deciding in too many cases that the Negro does not "understand" the constitution and that a white man, even though he be an ignorant white foreigner, with recently acquired citizenship, does "understand" it. In a recent article President Hadley, of Yale University, covers the whole truth when he says: "We cannot make a law which shall allow the right exercise of a discretionary power." While discussing this matter, it would be unfair to the white people of the South and to my own race, if I were not perfectly frank. What interpretation does the outside world and the Negro put upon these "understanding" clauses? Either that they are meant to leave a loophole so that the ignorant white man can vote, or to prevent the educated Negro from voting. If this interpretation is correct in either case, the law is unjust. It is unjust to the white man because it takes away from him the incentive to prepare himself to become an intelligent voter. It is unjust to the Negro because it makes him feel that no matter how well he prepared himself in education for voting, he will be refused a vote through the operation of the "understanding" clause.'

These warnings went unheeded but had their accuracy as predictions proved by the voting statistics. The oligarchy had control of the electoral vote, the state governments and the South's representation in the federal government. Booker T. Washington's warning about the dwarfing of morals came true, as a few men used their power to manipulate the economy and ensure poverty, to govern so as to bring disrespect for law, and so to control the lives of people as to render them insecure and fearful.

Votes cast in the elections of Democratic Presidents since

Grover Cleveland show the wane and recent beginnings of an upsurge in the influence of the people in the government of the states of the South.

Democratic President	Election Year	Democratic Votes Cast in 11 Southern States	Per Cent of Democratic Votes Cast in U.S.	Per Cent of total vote cast in the United States
Grover Cleveland	1892	1,241,065	22.3	10.3
Woodrow Wilson	1912	1,031,987	16.4	7.4
F. D. Roosevelt	1932	4,752,580	20.8	12.5
Harry Truman	1948	2,557,402	10.6	5.3
John F. Kennedy	1960	5,185,119	15.2	7.6

The total vote cast in 1912 was smaller than the vote cast in 1892 in Alabama, Arkansas, Georgia, Louisiana, North Carolina, South Carolina and Virginia. In 1892, 232,757 votes were cast in Alabama of which 138,138 were cast for Cleveland. In 1912 only 117,879 votes were cast but the percentage of the vote that was Democratic had increased from 59.3 to 69.9.

Beginning with the Roosevelt administration changes have come in the South that inescapably threaten to diminish the political influence of the oligarchy. The most significant harbinger of change in voting in the South was the 1944 Supreme Court decision that forbade restriction of the primaries of the Democratic Party in the South to white voters only. Payment of a poll tax as a qualification for voting has been removed in all but five states. Even in these States: Alabama, Arkansas, Mississippi, Texas and Virginia, the poll tax is no longer cumulative as had been the case that required a voter to pay the taxes assessed for each year since he became of voting age.

Despite the reform of voting laws, the proportion of the population of voting age that votes in the South remains smaller than the proportion in the rest of the United States. In the last three presidential elections the following percentages of the population of voting age cast ballots:

State	Percentage of Potential Voters that Cast Ballots.		
	Election Year:		
	1952	1956	1960
United States	62·7	65.2	63·3
Alabama	25	28	31
Arkansas	38	26	41
Florida	50	61	50
Louisiana	40	32	45
Georgia	31	31	30
Mississippi	24	20	25
North Carolina	52	50	53
South Carolina	31	27	31
Tennessee	46	47	50
Texas	43	41	42
Virginia	31	34	33

Economic changes in the South have been stimulated by federal aid programmes and subsidies which the oligarchy sought to manipulate to their satisfaction. Investment capital from outside the South has come to finance development of industries that also had to accept restrictions imposed by states and municipalities. Only the oligarchy expected that either 'Big Government' or 'Big Business' would long suffer being hampered in their efficient operations by archaic political rules that supported discriminatory customs.

Control of the prerogatives of Negroes in politics, in employment, and in other areas of living has been the oligarchy's self-chosen test of its powers which, by the same token, becomes an index to the attrition of its powers when that control is impinged upon. A succession of infringements on the regulation of the prerogatives of Negroes by the oligarchy has occurred in the following order:

1941 President Franklin D. Roosevelt issued Executive Order 8802 establishing a Fair Employment Practices Committee to insure the equitable participation of Negroes in the prosecution of World War II.

1944 Special disabilities imposed on Negro voting by the White Primary 'laws' were removed by the United States Supreme Court.

1946 President Harry S. Truman created the President's Committee on Civil Rights in Executive Order 9708.

1955 U.S. Supreme Court ordered racial segregation in public schools ended.

1957 President Dwight D. Eisenhower orders federal troops to Little Rock, Arkansas which stunned the oligarchy as a warning that federal authority can be backed by a police power.

1957 The United States Congress enacts a Civil Right Law.

1961 The Attorney General of the United States orders U.S. Marshals to Montgomery, Alabama to preserve law and order when state and local police authority failed to act in a racial conflict situation.

How the oligarchy wantonly abused the power in which it had entrenched itself and how it continues desperately to resist attrition of that power are described in the following chapters.

CHAPTER I

The Changing Southern Landscape

SINCE 1940 there has been activity on Southern farm lands more furious than spring ploughing after a long wet winter. Seeds of grasses have been sown over acres on which for a century, more or less, plough and hoe destroyed grass that cotton might thrive. Faithful trained mules who had names were scrapped, along with the crude farm implements they had drawn, and replaced by machines that could cultivate more acres in less time. On the outskirts of villages and towns factories were built in fields among the withered stalks that had borne last year's harvest. And, the reapers of last year's harvest were finished with harvesting. Ploughmen had been scrapped along with their ploughs and mules. In the new grasslands a lusher growth of oblong pattern marks sites of the demolished houses of people who have gone from the land.

Where cotton once grew on both sides of a road, now, for mile after mile, there are pastures and grazing cattle. Sometimes grass-covered terraces are a reminder that this was once a field in which row crops were grown.

In some places where cotton is still grown, cabins are no longer scattered about the fields in that expedient disarray that placed each family in the midst of the crop it was responsible for tilling. For tractors drawing gang ploughs, they were an inconvenience, and to aeroplanes spreading poison dust, they were a menace.

There are spots where the weatherworn cabins stand as they have been standing for decades and people seem to farm as they have been farming all their lives. Here the plantation system has apparently survived. Closer scrutiny shows that it really has not, despite the 'big house' standing as it has for decades and the grey cabins scattered as they have long been. Automobiles stand before the cabins and tractors are parked in sheds in the old mule lot. The commissary, traditional gathering place during idle hours, is shuttered and bleak-looking, deserted. Other things not readily discernible make the plantation in the 1960's significantly different from the plantation in 1940.

The many ploughmen trudging behind their mules talking to the beasts or relieving the boredom by singing or shouting their 'hollers' are gone. Instead, a few ploughmen ride tractors with colourful umbrellas to shield them from the sun and the only sound in the fields is the monotonous noise of the machines occasionally punctuated by the rasping clash of gears. In the autumn the cotton-harvesting machines, looking like grotesque red beetles, lumber among the cotton plants snatching the white fibre with steel claws. Trucks filled with raw cotton hurry along the highways to gins or loaded with burlap-covered bales hurry to market.

The highways, smooth belts of concrete or asphalt, have come too since 1930. They connect the cities to each other and the larger towns to cities. Markers point from the highway to the villages and small towns that the highways by-pass as they are no longer important to trade and commerce. The small towns and villages do have an importance however. They are the refuges for workers that the tractors and harvesters have pushed out of the fields. Big towns, little towns, and villages have grown since 1930. Small houses that have extended their boundaries are home for workers the farms have expelled and that city industries don't need.

The long-abused and misused lands of the South are faring better than the long-abused and misused people who have inhabited them. There have been no policies and scientific practices to ensure the constructive use of these people. Many of them who should be regarded as assets have been callously marked 'expendable'. This waste of human resources is the South's great unsolved problem. Soils in the South are being planned for in terms of their highest and more constructive purpose, whether it be forest, grass, or field. None of the land is regarded as waste and expendable. For every acre there is a use that in time will prove to be an asset. Sleek, well-fed cows graze on hillsides where gaunt, ill-fed people once scratched for a meagre living. In fertile fields where children and their parents toiled without hope of security or comfort, machines sow, tend, and harvest bounteous crops.

The faces of the people too are a part of the landscape. Puzzlement, bewilderment and confusion are familiar expressions on the faces of the people. The farmer knows that things are happening to him and to the world with which he has been familiar. He has his own ideas about them. His children and many of his former neighbours have gone away. As one farmer stated, 'I know more folks in Fort Wayne, Indiana, now than I do here. When I go to see my children in Fort Wayne, I also see all my old friends that used to live here.'

Another old farmer was bewildered and somewhat indignant about what was happening to the people among whom he had lived. 'The man what rented the old Newell Plantation,' he reported, 'done nailed up twenty houses! Yes sir, the people had to get out; some of them didn't have no place to go. Never been before in this here part of the country that a man couldn't get a piece of land to work. But this man rented the place and come here with two tractors—say him and his boy gonna work all of it theyself. All around here landlords buying tractors and the folks is just uncertain; they just can't be sure they gonna have a crop next year or they ain't.'

As expected, neighbourhood and community life suffers along with these changes. Schools have been closed and the picturesque little buildings are rotting away. A woman pointed to a church building, with peeling paint, that leaned precariously on three heavy timbers and commented, 'That's our church but we don't have no regular preacher, just a little Sunday School mostly. So many folks gone from here we ain't got but a handful of members and can't support no church.'

The South is feeling the impact of a complex revolution. In one form the industrial revolution finally came to one of the last strongholds of hand labour and family enterprise. Everywhere and at whatever time it came, the industrial revolution brought serious enough problems. But its coming to the South coincided with an ideological revolution that in itself presented serious problems. The Rust Brothers invention of the mechanical cotton harvester had to get into production but the New Deal agricultural policies went into effect immediately.

Few people realized in the summer of 1933 that more than cotton plants were being ploughed up when three-fourths of the cotton growers destroyed cotton growing on ten and a half million acres of land. An economic order and a system of social relationships were being uprooted. The Old South did not go with some wind; it was ploughed up, or under, in the summer of 1933. Payment for the plough-up was no settlement; it was an unsettlement destined to change the Southern landscape.

The agrarian economy, influenced as it has been by many changes, is no longer dominant in the South. There are recently built factories in Southern cities and surprising modern buildings are on the outskirts of villages and sometimes stand in isolation in the open country. These are not new industries or new companies entering into competition with older companies. They are additional plants of Ford Motor Company, International Harvester, Dow Chemical, St Regis Paper. Some are replacements of obsolete plants in the older industrial areas outside of the South. A new economic and social force has been introduced into the South with the investment of capital and development of productive enterprises by big business corporations. Another economic and social force also came as a part of industrialization—organized labour. The Southern oligarchy will hardly be able to keep promises made to industry to attract it to the South. One of these promises, characteristic of the Southern oligarchy, was an advertisement in national magazines by the government of Mississippi offering industries that located there the advantage of 'cheap, tractable, native white labour'.

Now on the Southern landscape there are factories and the villages about them to house industrial workers. An eye-catching view is to be had by the early morning traveller who passes through one of the areas where a plant has been located so as to employ workers who live on farms. At a distance of fifty miles from such a plant automobiles begin coming from by-roads, empty into the highway and flow as a stream to the factory.

Changes in the landscape are symbolic. The tension and conflict, the insecurity and unrest, the hope and anticipation, the insistence on preservation of the old and the clamour for something new, all are behind the symbols. To understand what has happened and is happening in the South today deeper comprehension is needed of what it was like before it knew the disturbances of war, depression, agricultural mechanization and reform, and industrialization.

Over this area an oligarchy has ruled for eighteen years. Never before since it took power has it been so sorely beset. The Supreme Court decisions on segregation would not be so serious a threat to it if the decisions did not come at a time of change in the climate of national opinion. That change of climate is not hospitable to THE SOUTH as an ideology. New economic flora and new social fauna are altering the Southern landscape in this climate. The oligarchy now struggles desperately to retain a power that has become seriously threatened as government by the people sprouts among the other new growths in this land.

CHAPTER II

1910: Flourishing Bitterweed

THE census of 1910 showed that the cotton-production system in the South had reached maturity with all of its distinctive characteristics fully formed. In the cotton fields, the cotton market-towns, in the full-blown system and its institutions, the evils that would destroy it were firmly fixed. Here was rooted that social weed that was to stifle the economy and make of democracy in the South a dwarf growth. Circumstances would make the oligarchy that towering weed.

Profile: 1910

The South had 32 per cent of the nation's people, 15 per cent of its urban population and 46 per cent of its rural population. The rural population was 78 per cent of the total Southern population, in contrast to 41 per cent in the North and 51 per cent in the West. There were only nine cities in the South with 100,000 population.

There were 2,620,391 farms in the South with an average value of $2,900 in contrast to $9,500 in the North and $12,000 in the West. All farm property on Southern farms had an average value of $25 an acre. It had 99.7 per cent of all the land in the United States planted to cotton and in 1909, 65.9 per cent of all money spent on fertilizer in the United States was spent in the South. The South had 72 per cent of all the farm mules, 89 per cent of all the Negroes, and 65 per cent of all tenant farmers in the United States.

The new system, supplanting the slave system, had come of age by 1910, after several decades of trying at adjustment. The shift from a slave labour system to a free labour system in southern agriculture was made in the utmost confusion. Many wars ending in conquest gave to the enriched conquerors a rationale for impressing the labour of the conquered to exploit their newly-gained economic resources. To the contrary, the Civil War left the agricultural lands of the South in possession of an impoverished land-owning class among the defeated. The only resource of this group was land which was worth little without labour or money to hire labour.

The slaves who had been freed in the course of the war found themselves, at its close, desperately in need of the essentials for sustaining life—shelter, food and clothing. The imperative of the situation was that former master and former slave established some sort of co-operation for their mutual benefit. This co-operation involved the former slaves returning to the lands they had tilled and there to make use of familiar skills in the production of familiar crops. The former masters reassumed the management and supervisory functions with which they were familiar. The agreement of former masters and former slaves to resume their productive functions was necessary to the resumption of the production of the South's staple crops to feed raw materials to the North's industries. The conditions of this agreement involved a farm tenancy system.

Statutes enacted and incorporated in the common law of the states following the Civil War were not invented for that period. The tenancy laws of the Southern states are basically British common law and in their present provisions date from the reign of Queen Anne who ruled England between 1702 and 1714. The landlord's rights and prerogatives were safe-guarded, while the tenant had few rights that were recognized at all to be safe-guarded.

These laws fitted well the political mood and temper of the post-Civil War period. Restoration to political power of the former slaveholder class, who had been joined by a new land-owning group interested in immediate profits from investment in land ensured a continuance of these archaic laws. The former slaveholders felt a need to have tenants in a position as close to the old slave status as was practicable. The new commercial farmers cared little whether the labour they used in exploiting their lands was black or was made up of whites who now came off the infertile lands to compete for the opportunity to till the

rich lands. There was a mood of urgency on the part of landowners to get profit quickly, and laws that gave them the control
and domination of labour appeared to be essential to efficient and
profitable operation of the South's agricultural lands. No instrument could serve their purpose better than oral agreements
which the provisions of the old common law governed, im-
plicitly but legally.

Volumes and pages in more volumes have been written
describing the evils of the Reconstruction era in the South and
most of these accounts conclude with exultation over the
wresting of short-lived power from 'scalawags, carpetbaggers,
and niggers' to return it where it belonged, to the old planter
aristocracy. This picture of the redemption of the fine old
South is something about which romanticists grow weepily
sentimental. What really happened was the usurpation of power
by new financial and political interests, which had by 1910 ruthlessly entrenched themselves so as to go about a shameless
exploitation of the South's natural and human resources. The
men who represented these interests loved neither land nor
men and knew not honour.

Jauntily, this new ilk claimed for its regime the happy sobri-
quet, 'The New South', whose claims and promises were presented far and near in the clarion voice of Henry W. Grady. The
Southern historian, Francis Butler Simpkins, in his *A History of
the South*, takes a jaundiced view of the vaunted 'New South',
saying of it:

'Undoubtedly, Grady and those who applauded him were
motivated by the thought that reconciliation with the North
would bestow benefits upon all classes of Southerners. Their
actions, however, were not entirely idealistic; behind their fine
phrases was the desire for private gain. As their first move,
Bourbon politicians furnished the prestige of great names;
merchants and bankers supplied the money. Next the politicians and their journalist friends took action that had the
earmarks of scalawagism. Northern businessmen, a sort of
second generation of carpetbaggers, invaded every Southern
state in search of profits, offering the gospel of material
prosperity. . . .'

Efforts were made to improve the South's economy by industrialization, but cotton continued to be the basis of the
economy. The key to economic profits became the new agricultural credit system that Southern bankers and merchants
had engineered. The report of the Comptroller of the Currency
for 1915 showed that 343 national banks in the Southern states
charged 12 per cent interest, while only thirty banks in Northern states charged such interest. There were reported banks in
the South whose interest rates were even higher than 12 per
cent.

In many cotton fields virtual slavery was restored. The flag-
rancy of holding men in bondage was investigated by the
secret service during the administration of Theodore Roosevelt,
and the reports led to an investigation of peonage by a committee of Congress in 1908.

In order to manipulate the economy, it was essential to control
government. Dramatizing and exaggerating the horrors of reconstruction, the politicians used the Negro as whipping-boy and
in legislating his disfranchisement also disfranchised many
whites, kept the electorate small, and achieved control of government. By 1910 the 'New Southerners' had legislated themselves
into a security by amendments to state constitutions which disfranchised a large proportion of the electorate. Less than 28 per
cent of the total male population of voting age in the South
voted in the presidential election of 1912. 'Pitchfork' Ben
Tillman could, in the decade before 1910, proudly, if rudely,
announce on the floor of the United States Senate that the whites
'rose in righteousness and right. We took government; we
stuffed the ballot boxes, we bulldozed the niggers and we shot
'em. And we are not ashamed of it.' The New South had come
to power and that power was used so that all the Cotton South
came to suffer from it.

The record of personal chicanery and corruption in political
office extended to high places. The Ben Tillman quoted above
achieved such a cloudy reputation for personal shady dealings
that President Theodore Roosevelt pointedly cancelled an invitation to him to dine at the White House. Vardaman of
Mississippi was sued for misuse of public monies. These instances, from many, of malfeasance and use of public office for

B

personal gain were not the most serious offences of the rulers of
the 'New South'. They were guilty of greater crimes against
the people.

There came into being in the South the chain gang and the
convict lease system. In 1910 when ten Southern states were compared to ten Northern states, the jail population in the Southern
states was 29,726 and that in the Northern states 19,730; convictions for homicide in the South were 3,540 compared to 965
in the North. Booker T. Washington was to cry out against the
convict lease system, the contract labour laws, and the spree of
arresting Negroes.

In 1910-11 the Rockefeller Sanitary Commission entered the
South on a mission of hookworm control. A survey of fifty-two
counties in ten states between 1910 and 1914 showed 57.8 per
cent of the children examined to be infested with hookworm.
Summary information on health for this period is not available
because of all of the Southern states only North Carolina was in
the registration area in 1910.

Education was poorly supported and the school was a feeble
institution in the South. There was no eager effort to bring up
a better-thinking and better-trained generation. As late as 1918
per capita expenditures for public schools in the ten lowest
states in the nation, all Southern states, averaged $2.93 while
the ten highest, none Southern, averaged $12.40. Even so, the
funds for Negro children in the South were diverted to white
children and defended by the rationalization that education
made Negroes lawless.

Such was the 'New South' arriving at its apogee around 1910.
1912 was approaching, when Southern politicians would control
the congress under a Democratic president. The politicians had
achieved an easily manipulated governmental machinery and
used it to enact laws that would serve their far from admirable
purposes. Among these laws were those that provided for corrupting the economy. Public institutions and public services,
where they existed, only barely survived, starved for support as
they were.

In this period folk commentary on the economic and political
systems got widely circulated. These comments had the character
of sardonic humour that is still puzzling to people who simply

cannot understand the persistent cheerfulness of Negroes in such circumstances. Expressed in rhyme and story, these comments are now hoary and frazzled, but bear quoting here to indicate how people at the bottom of the economic and social scale saw the system. They were aware of the change in their value as the slave system gave way to the tenant system. Under slavery they had value and were protected, as valuable possessions are protected. They came to interpret the philosophy of the new class of masters, who had no investment in them as persons thus:

> *' Kill a mule,*
> *Buy another*
> *Kill a nigger,*
> *Hire another.'*

They felt that these new Southerners were concerned only about their labour. So long as they could work, the landlords had no care about their well-being. There was no appeal to be made from a government of landlords or agents of landlords.

That they could laugh at the exploitation about which they were helpless may be strange human behaviour, but laugh they did and took pains to put their laughter into rhyme. One of the universally quoted jingles was:

> *' A 'aught's a 'aught*
> *And a figger's a figger*
> *All for the white*
> *None for the nigger.'*

Almost as common in their quoting are stories such as this one:

' How I let him cheat me? I didn't let him. He just did. I kept books on everything, I took up on credit and all the cotton I made. When settlement time I take my book with me and he tell me I'm $364 in debt. I tell him my book say I got $430 coming to me. He say he don't go by my book; he go by his'n.'

' I say I'm gonna get him this year. When I go to settle he bring out his book and say, " Joe, you took up a thousand and forty dollars credit. You made twenty-one bales of cotton. That came to $945. You got $95 coming, here it is " '

Then I say, "That all I owe, Boss?"
He say, "Yeah, you done pretty good this year."
Then I say, "Well, I can go ahead and sell these two bales I got in the barn."
He say, "Wait! Wait a minute and let me figger this again!"
I don't get but that $95.'

Without schooling and the reading and figuring they needed they were at the mercy of the 'figurer'. Even if they could read and count, the laws governing their status had been written against them. If they were unquestionably right in figure and according to law, the ethics of the 'New South', and the customs the new Southerners formed on the basis of these ethics, included the understanding that no self-respecting white man would take the word of a Negro when he was in a dispute with a white man. Those who were morally bound to take the white man's version included jurymen and judges.

The system in the 'New South' produced its inevitable social consequences. The entirely sympathetic but discerning Southern journalist, Virginius Dabney, in *Below the Potomac* reports:

'. . . the average white Southern sharecropper or other marginal worker comes of sturdy Anglo-Saxon yeoman stock, that many of these under-privileged people are proud and self-reliant, if given half a chance to break out of the cycle of poverty and disease which has held them for so long in its vice-like grip, and that about all they need is rudimentary medical attention, and some instruction in agricultural and dietary fundamentals, together with enough credit to enable them to shake off the shackles of the one-crop "furnishing-merchant" system. Until the New Deal attacked this situation by means of Federal legislation, no comprehensive effort to ameliorate it had been made. While many of these "poor whites" are undoubtedly beyond redemption, a decided majority are capable of marked improvement, once they are made physically whole and educationally receptive. . .'

and describes

'. . . the hundreds and thousands of migratory tenants and 'croppers, both white and black, who are almost constantly

on the move in the cotton belt, dragging after them a few
dented pots and pans, a few sticks of battered furniture, and
a half a dozen or more ragged children . . . over one-third
of whom move every year from tumble-down shacks to tumble-
down shacks, carrying their irresponsible farming methods
with them, and exhausting the soil to the limit of their abilities, since they have no incentive to do anything else.'

CHAPTER III

1910-1930: Burgeon and Blight

UNTIL the decade following 1910 neither the economic nor the political order in the South knew serious disturbances. The problems of the South were regarded as chronic and under control. The nemesis of the cotton plant was water—too much or too little of it at the wrong time. Drought and flood were accepted as the natural risks of cotton growing. The fluctuations of cotton prices from year to year were the risks of the market. The production system was stabilized. The political pattern had also achieved stability. In the Republican administrations of Mc-Kinley and Theodore Roosevelt, 1896-1908, occasional gestures were made towards the Negroes to punctuate the oratorical claims of being the party of Abraham Lincoln. So long as the Republicans controlled the national government, the oligarchy might be troubled by a sense of insecurity but its fears were groundless. The Republican Party did not reconsider the compromise of 1876 through which Rutherford B. Hayes secured the Presidency and the Southern oligarchy gained political control of the South. In 1912 Woodrow Wilson, of Virginia and Georgia by way of New Jersey, became President of the United States. The Democratic Party controlled the national government. The Southern oligarchy was relieved of any apprehension about its security.

Economically and politically the South was to enjoy a burgeoning of such headiness that a spirit of recklessness on the part of the oligarchy would be engendered. For its irresponsibility in success it would face grave reckoning. Little did the South realize that in its apogee there were the seeds of its nadir. The war-boom it welcomed was the boom phase of a prosperity-depression cycle. The political power it enjoyed was the power phase of a dominance-submission cycle. The economic bust was scheduled for the decade following 1920, and political submission was scheduled for the decade following 1930. Over-expansion of cotton production would literally reduce the economic system to shambles by 1930.

World War I brought to realization the circumstance of increase in price accompanying increase in production. The wishful thinkers were wildly elated and ignored the simple fact that this war economy would not long outlast the war. In 1924 there were thirty-nine million acres of land planted to cotton. This was an increase of 22 per cent over the acreage so planted in 1909. Every available acre of land was sown to cotton. One disillusioned farmer commented after the boom had passed that, 'We planted cotton on land that would grow cotton just as the kitchen floor would if you covered it with enough fertilizer.' Prices of land rose and planters bought more land at the high prices. Small farmers mortgaged the farms they owned as security for additional land. Confidently they expected cotton to reach a market price of one dollar a pound and they would pay off their debts with 'dollar-a-pound' cotton. Some believed this so strongly that they held harvested cotton off the market to sell and 'make a killing' when cotton reached a dollar-a-pound. Sharecroppers bought mules and ploughs at high prices on credit and became managing tenants.

The boom carried cotton as a cash crop to its logical, if unwise, conclusion. The old-fashioned, self-sufficient plantation disappeared. All land in cotton! No feed crops for animals. No food crops for people. Grow cotton and buy what you need. Tenants 'lived out of the commissary'. The plantation stores charged exorbitant prices and added usurious interest to the cost. The tenants didn't care. They got what they wanted and the landlords encouraged them to load themselves up. The landlords' reasoning was that the less the share of cotton harvested due to the tenant, the more for the landlord. There was an additional reason for this prodigality of the landlord: the tenants had to be kept satisfied because their labour was needed to grow the precious 'white stuff'.

For the first time since 1880 the planters were concerned about having an ample labour supply. Just when they needed more and more labour, the war took young men into the army, and the expanding industries in the North sought to meet their needs from the Negroes in the South. Cotton planters were determined to give every inducement to labourers to remain in the cotton fields and to place every obstacle in the way of those who were lured by the attractions offered by northern industries.

The planters were determined not to let labour escape from them to the North. Labour agents who came recruiting for northern industries met harsh receptions. Some were beaten, some were fined, some were jailed, and some were just run out of the county. Local peace officers met all trains stopping in the villages or at the whistle stops; labour recruiters were discouraged from getting off, and no potential industrial labourers dared to try to get on.

Other booms have perhaps been as disastrous as this one, but none could have been more fundamentally destructive to an economic system. All of this plenty ended with ruin. Literally millions of acres of farmland had been 'mined', exhausted of fertility. The productive system was so geared to a single cash crop that it went on planting that crop as if under a sense-depriving compulsion. By 1930 the whole cotton structure had collapsed.

If the economic system can be said to have gone berserk, the same may be said of the political system. John Hope Franklin, in his *From Slavery to Freedom*, reports that in the first Congress during the Wilson administration at least twenty bills were introduced advocating segregation of the races in public carriers in the District of Columbia, the exclusion of Negroes from commissions in the army and navy, separate accommodations for Negro and white federal employees, and exclusion of immigrants of Negro descent. The President obliged the Southern wing of his party by using the executive power to ends it sought. He issued an executive order segregating Negro federal employees in the use of government eating and rest-room facilities. The various departments of the executive branch of the government responsible to the President did grievous hurt to Negroes.

America's entry into the war provided opportunity to impress upon the Negro what his place was in the nation. Negroes were barred from the marine corps. They were admitted to the navy only in the ranks that made of them menials in uniform. The highest-ranking Negro officer in the army of the United States, Colonel Charles Young, West Point graduate, was mandatorily retired because of 'high blood pressure'. This impressive soldier sought to dramatize his physical fitness by riding horseback from Ohio to Washington to appeal against the retirement. Southern Democrats would see no Negro have the rank to which Colonel Young was entitled in the American army. Before the decade closed seventy Negroes, ten of them in army uniform, were lynched in a single year. Twenty-five race riots occurred between June and December 1919.

The influence of the oligarchy may be seen in the fact that the Wilsonian ideology, that gave to World War I whatever aspect of idealism there came to be attached to it, did not, even by implication, include racial considerations. In this struggle between Europeans for power in Europe, brown and black colonial troops were used by the governments involved, but no assurances were offered to Senegalese, Indians, or American Negroes concerning post-war awards. American Negro soldiers were treated as were the other dark-skinned troops—like impressed and paid mercenaries. American Negro troops were to be subjected to the unhappy experience of hearing bitter words of wisdom from a leading Negro selected and sent to speak to them before they left Europe. His message was to the effect that they should expect the old order to be maintained at home despite any different adventures and experiences they had known in Europe. Bitter though the message from home was, it came from a sequence of events on the home front and was destined to be supported by happenings after the war. In southern small towns welcomes were given to returned Negro veterans in formal meetings which were addressed by some member of the oligarchy who told them that the home folks were proud of them, *but* the better part of civilian valour was to get out of uniform and get to work as quickly as possible. They were told that the white people, who were their neighbours, took affectionate care of the Negro who knew his place and kept it.

Much has been written about the Harding-Coolidge era in the 1920's. Sometimes described as the 'Jazz Age' characterized by the 'flapper' and the 'gin mill', it was basically a period

B*

of good times and complacency. America was taking little notice
of its chronic ills or deep-rooted problems for which there would
come an inevitable day of reckoning. The Republican national
administration left the South to its own devices. New York's
Harlem and Chicago's South Side offered Negroes a freedom
such as they had not known in the South. The narrow limits of
this new-found freedom were not immediately realized by the
Negroes. There were riots, but they were riots in which Negroes
could fight back. They would learn that the places in the northern cities where they could live were restricted ghettos. There
were discriminations in the places they could go and the jobs
they could hold, but these would be found first by the middle-
class Negroes. There may have been bars about their place in the
North, but they were not shackled. So they gaily sang, 'I'd
rather be a lamp-post on State Street than mayor down home.'

'Down home' things were such that hundreds of thousands
went North in the decade of the twenties to join their kin and
friends, who had slipped away during wartime. Contradictions
in the South in this period provide a rather confusing picture.
Though Negroes had a share in the prosperity they could not
freely enjoy the money that came to them. A silk shirt, one of
the then uncommon automobiles, or a pretentious new house
were in too many instances interpreted as symbols of a Negro
'getting out of his place'. A white mob might take on the
responsibility for setting the perspective of such a Negro
straight. In politics the Republican 'Black and Tan' organizations (mostly black) continued to function every four years. Stal-
wart politicians among Negroes were Bob Church of Tennessee,
Perry Howard of Mississippi and Ben J. Davis of Georgia. Some
of these, especially Church, had an understanding with the
Democratic oligarchy. The Democratic Crump machine and
Church's Republican machine enjoyed a productive co-operation.
Crump's ability to deliver the Shelby County vote was due in
part to Church's Republicans voting as Crump wanted them to in
state and local elections, while voting for the Republican candidate for President.

Bewildered Negroes in the North found themselves as much
of an immigrant first generation as did any group of Europeans who had come to America. Consigned to ghettos and

rebuffed at every turn in these strange cities, they milled about in confusion. Some of them paraded behind Marcus Garvey admiring his cocked hat with its waving plumes. They listened to his nonsense about an African homeland. They were wandering in a psychological wilderness. They would reach the homeland, but not in some distant illusory place. The ships of Garvey's Black Star Line rotting in New York Harbour would not bear them to any African shore.

None of the escapes imagined in the 1920's would prove to be a haven from a hostile America. No shade of black nationalism would provide an avenue of escape. The formula for escape from disadvantage had been available for as long as the formula for Southern economic redemption had been. It simply remained to be used. It called for the hard reality of political action. As had all other American immigrant groups, the Negroes had to go through a period of preparation to exercise political influence in their own interest and in the interest of their oppressed fellows, who had not been fortunate enough to migrate.

In retrospect, that period when Negroes were in the psychological wilderness, preparing to assert themselves, is a most interesting one. Negro intellectuals, enjoying comparative freedom in the northern ghettos, gave to Negroes a sense of pride and worth through poem, song, and story. The National Urban League gave them a sense of economic opportunism as well as hope for economic opportunity. The National Association for the Advancement of Coloured People gave them a sense of direction through concerted action, through public relations techniques, and through persistent legal action. What was to be done for Negroes in America had to be done by the Negro immigrants in the North. To do it they had to gain organizational strength and political power there. In the Northern cities, they registered Republican and added their votes to the strength of the big city machines.

The first national political figure the northern migration produced was himself an immigrant from Alabama. In the terrible Chicago riot in 1919 he distinguished himself by organizing the rescue of the Negro stockyard workers who were cut off from their South Side homes. Earlier, he had gained some experience in leadership as an alderman, but had lost his place in disgrace charged with taking petty graft. Having been strengthened by this new experience, he became a spokesman for the Negroes of Chicago. In 1928 he won a seat in Congress with the campaign slogan, 'Fight for Oscar; Oscar fights for you.' Oscar DePriest from Chicago was the first Negro to sit in Congress since White of North Carolina left there in 1901.

The migrants and their leaders were to find a place in New York, Pittsburgh, Cleveland, Chicago, and Detroit in the 1920's. The place they found for themselves in the North was relatively unimportant compared to the change they were destined to make in the South. Their presence and their doings in the North ensured that the fortunes of the South would be a matter of self-interest to the two major political parties, and consequently of the federal government.

James Weldon Johnson of Florida and Walter White from Georgia went about building a strong organization around the NAACP nucleus. The National Urban League was the organization of the Virginians—Eugene Kinckle Jones, T. Arnold Hill, and Charles S. Johnson. Robert S. Abbott from Savannah was making his *Chicago Defender* the first nationally circulated Negro weekly to influence public opinion.

While the Negroes were moving towards strength in the North, the whites in the South were going on a rampage. The Ku Klux Klan, mightiest oppressive force the South ever marshalled, spread over the South's boundaries to gain strength in Indiana, Illinois, and Missouri. The Klan, hooded and sheeted, marched on its mission of intolerance and persecution everywhere, even through the campus of Tuskegee Institute past Booker T. Washington's grave. Those who remembered could think on his warning about unbridled power and the irresponsible use of it 'dwarfing the morals of the white man in the South'. Persecuting Jews, Catholics, and Negroes, the Klan played its part in the self-destructive Democratic rejection of Alfred E. Smith. The election of Herbert Hoover in 1928 marked the ebb-tide of the political power of the Southern Democrats. The South was already in a depression which was only to be intensified by the 1929 debacle.

1930 found the South blighted both economically and politically. Salvation would come, but not as restoration. Internal and external circumstances precluded restoration. Cotton as king, the plantation system as tyrant, and the oligarchy as unchallenged power had come to their dynastic ends. The South could not redeem itself economically. It required help from outside to work out its problems. The formula for their solution was available. It had been available before Henry Grady stated it in terms of the South's fields being green in winter, and a balance of agriculture and industry. With help this solution would have to be made in the South. The solution of the South's problems would not remain long in its own hands. It had shown itself to be politically irresponsible in a way that threatened not only the well-being of the South but that of the nation as well. The threat it represented to the Nation included the fortunes of the Democratic Party. The Democratic Party could redeem itself only by putting tight rein on its Southern wing. Hindsight shows that what happened in these two decades was the seed from which a different social growth would come.

CHAPTER IV

1930-1950: New Growth Alongside the Withering Stalk

A T few times in history have there been so many system-shaking events crowded into a generation. An order-shattering economic depression followed by an order-reshaping mobilization for war could be expected to produce enduring changes. America's internal policies for economic recovery and those for prosecution of the war were guided by a philosophy of destructive import for the oligarchy. The 'Roosevelt Revolution' and the industrial revolution coming together were to do many things to the South and southern people—white and black. The move of these forces would not be stayed by the oligarchy. They proved too big for the oligarchy to cope with, even when it exerted itself mightily to join what it could not beat.

The political campaign of 1932 gave muted warning of what was to come. For the oligarchy there had been four years to mull over its desertion of Governor Smith. For its support, President Hoover rewarded it with the freedom to exercise power within its hegemony. For this the oligarchy needed no licence. In addition, however, they could take comfort from the fact that Hoover showed little sympathy for the Negro's cause. Roscoe Conklin Simmons, the popular Negro orator, whose voice was a familiar one in the Republican hustings made public appeal to Mr Hoover during the 1932 campaign. 'Speak, Mr President, Speak', Simmons pleaded, seeking words to assure the Negro voters that the Republican Party was yet 'the party of Abraham Lincoln'. No word, no reassuring whisper came from the Republican candidate. The word of hope was to come later from an unexpected source—strong words in the mellifluous voice of the Democrat, Franklin D. Roosevelt.

The Republican Party garnered an estimated three-fourths of the Negro vote in the 1932 election. The inauguration of President Roosevelt on March 4, 1933 was a moment of happy anticipation for the oligarchy as the 'Southern wing' of the Democratic party. The oligarchs might well have expected a return of the halcyon days they had known under Woodrow Wilson. They had no premonition that Roosevelt would cast an ominous shadow, from which they could not escape in their being and doings. Certainly they did not dream that the President's wife would prove to be an accusing presence at their every banquet, or haunt their domain, shedding light on its open secrets. The President would begin by branding the South as 'The Nation's Economic Problem Number One', and proceed to brand stalwarts of the oligarchy, like Senator George of Georgia, his administration's political problem number one.

Despite President Roosevelt's hearty assurance that the American people 'had nothing to fear itself', the oligarchy was soon beset by the ultimate in fears. Its fortunes were entwined with those of a leadership determined to break it to harness for the drawing of a cargo of economic and political policies antagonistic to its peculiar interests. The prospect of bare political troughs as punishment for baulking was a frustrating thought. The oligarchy soon realized that it had to deal with a President, leader of its own party, who had few qualms about using his considerable powers to further the ends of his convictions. With political deftness, President Roosevelt sought to direct members of the oligarchy along lines of positive action that would employ their fine skills and enhance their stature. There were, and are, men of great intellectual powers among their members. They could serve the nation well if their talents were used for the common good, instead of being dissipated in furthering the interests of the oligarchy. Franklin D. Roosevelt gave these men responsibilities, which they lived up to so as to enter the ranks of America's eminent statesmen. Men like Cordell Hull, Hugo L. Black, and Maury Maverick were esteemed and honoured. A Bilbo or a Cotton Ed Smith could persist in demagoguery with full knowledge they would know only the back of Mr Roosevelt's hand. They could choose to play Mississippi or

South Carolina penny ante, but they did so knowing that no cards would be dealt them in the big game.

Cotton Ed could make himself ridiculous if he wanted to by stomping out of the National Democratic Convention in 1936, when the Reverend Marshall Shepherd prayed over that body, but he could do nothing more effective than sputter when the same Reverend Shepherd was appointed Recorder of Deeds for the District of Columbia. Theodore Bilbo could rant about sending Negroes back to Africa, while the only person headed towards repatriation, Bilbo, was returned to his Mississippi homeland by the Senate.

The oligarchy was not uprooted but it was neutralized. Rendered impotent in its own party, it had to seek common cause with conservative Republicans to have influence on legislation.

The 'New and Fair' deals of the twenty years of Democratic administration of the country left the South markedly different from what it had been in 1930.

A bankrupt South was examined by experts to verify what was already obvious—the South lacked the resources, the skill and the imagination to put its economy in a state of healthy productivity. Its people were, and long had been, 'ill-fed, ill-clothed, and ill-housed'. So long as these people were ill-employed and ill-paid, their clothing, feeding, and shelter would remain substandard. What was offered by the Roosevelt administration to relieve this state of affairs was not welcomed by the oligarchy, but it could make face-saving boasts that it got its share. The portion for the people of the South was ear-marked for them; it was intended to be a good share.

The sad plight of the Southern farmer along with that of other farmers required immediate attention. 43 per cent of the employed people in the South were engaged in agriculture in 1930 as compared to 15 per cent of the employed outside of the South. The programme of the AAA (Agricultural Adjustment Administration) in the first year of its operation increased the cash income from cotton and tobacco in the South by 500 million dollars. Other agencies were created by the Roosevelt administration to give attention to special aspects of the farm problem. The programme underwent modifications and the names of agencies were changed from time to time, but the reforms were worked at continuously. The Rural Resettlement Administration, the Production Credit Administration, the Civilian Conservation Corps, the Soil Conservation Service, the Rural Electrification Administration, and the Production Management Administration were all agencies developed to improve the lot of farmers. From the first they encountered difficulties with the oligarchy in carrying on their work.

All the way, year after year, there was foot-dragging if not actual sabotage of the programmes of these agencies in the South. Especially did they resist solutions to the South's problems that failed to include modifications taking into account their special concerns. The oligarchy, from the top down to its local community representatives, opposed the absence of racial differentials in the several programmes. This opposition had some success through the manner in which the programmes were administered at the local level. Every policy statement and procedural directive coming out of Washington was strained through local customs. The dominant Southerners wanted to enjoy salvation but they were not happy to see benefits go to Negroes and the poor whites.

When crop acreages were reduced in compliance with the AAA programme, the landowners did not respect the letter or spirit of the law and proceed to allocate the land to remain in cultivation equitably among the tenants. Various subterfuges were used to avoid compliance. Some landlords changed the status of tenants to that of wage-labourers, so as to take away their claim to equity in the cash bounties the programme provided. In some cases tenants were simply taken out of production as land was taken out. Twenty years later, local administrators of the Production Management Administration simply did not inform the small farmers of subsidies available, and distributed the quotas allocated to the area among the big farmers. When regulation enforcement depended upon policing by local community representatives of the oligarchy, there was simply no enforcement. The only effective control of the programme was in the fear of the spot checks made from Washington.

There were criticisms of the plans for farmhouses on the resettlement projects, on the grounds that to give Negroes houses with bath tubs and electric lights would spoil them.

One of the chronic problems in the South has been production credit at reasonable cost. The Production Credit Administration, with interest rates around 4 per cent, offered such credit. The banks charged 8 per cent in some areas and private lenders 10 per cent. Interviews with landlords show that they charged their tenants 18 to 20 per cent. One landlord explained to an interviewer, 'Hell, I don't charge no interest; it's against the law. You can't get but 8 per cent. I charge 25 per cent manager's fees and service costs.' Many of the farmers who needed the service did not get the information on what was available. A Negro county agent of the Extension Service defended his failure to inform his clients of the low-cost credit available to them, 'The bankers in this county got power; I'm not going around talking about production credit and get them against me.'

Enough Negroes benefited from the programme to give them a new hope. The federal government became 'The Government', in which they had confidence. Contributing to this sentiment was an incident that received wide publicity early in the Roosevelt régime. It was a joke to the Southern press, which printed it widely as an indication of the asininity of the Negro. A farmer named Sylvester telephoned the President and talked to him about the threatened loss of his mule because he couldn't pay a note due on the mule. Mr Roosevelt assured him that his mule and his productive security would be protected by one of the new agencies. To thousands of simple Negroes it was no joke. They had a President sensitive to their small but real concerns, a friend in the White House, and that was a new and exhilarating experience. Mrs Roosevelt's growing reputation for omnipresence and omniscience in the interest of their cause was a comfort to the Negroes and an annoyance to the oligarchy.

A Negro farmer who acquired ownership of a farm through the Farm Security Administration sat on his porch in Alabama and talked about the farm 'the Government gimme'. Finally he was asked, 'What do you mean the government gave this farm to you?'

'Well, you see it's like this,' he explained. 'My notes every year is less than I would have to pay to rent it. And let me tell you, I ain't thinking of no forty years to pay for it. 'Fore ten years I'm gonna have it paid for. Instead of paying a hundred dollars a year, three years ago I paid a thousand dollars. The next year I bought me a tractor so I didn't pay but the hundred. But the next year I paid another thousand. Last year I bought me a car but this year I'm gonna pay another thousand. The way I'm handling it it's just like they giving it to me.'

There were instances of tenants moving into ownership, representatives of the oligarchy permitting; despite the fact that mechanization of cotton harvesting was to preclude the South's becoming a region of small farms. In 1950 there were 571,393 fewer farms in the South than there were in 1930. Between 1940 and 1950, tenant farms decreased by 543,971. In 1930, 43.9 per cent of the farms in the South were owner operated. In 1950, 65.5 per cent were owner operated. The average size of farm in the South increased from 106 acres to 148 acres.

Farmers remaining on the land fared better than they had twenty years before. In 1940, 19 per cent of the farm dwellings were lighted by electricity; in 1950, 70 per cent were. In 1930 the average value of farm land and buildings were $3,800; in 1950 it was $8,600. The agricultural reform programme showed results. Infertile land was taken out of cultivation. Trees and grasses were planted on soil unsuited for the growing of row crops. Cattle growing became a major industry in the South. Planned production and diversified farming became the accepted practice. Better varieties and practices gave increased yields from familiar row crops.

The South also benefited from the industrial reforms the Roosevelt administration brought. Again the oligarchy was to be seen blocking here and dragging its feet there. CWA, PWA, WPA were welcomed, with reservations about the wages paid. To pay Negroes as much as whites were paid, and to pay both more than they were accustomed to receive, was regarded as interference. The Wagner Act and minimum-wage laws did things for the white textile workers that the agricultural reforms had done for Negroes. Negroes employed on the dirty jobs in tobacco manufacturing in the Carolinas and Virginia, and in the coal and steel industries, too, had fatter pay envelopes and better working conditions. A last straw was a no-discrimination clause in contracts for federally subsidized construction and production. The state of Mississippi simply refused to make any contracts with the federal government. Agricultural workers, new in factories, and craft organizations allied to the oligarchy, were obstacles, but slowly a new growth of labour unionism was rooted alongside the withering stalk of paternalism.

To share in benefits designed for all of the people, the proudest Negro had to humble himself and the humblest Negro to abase himself. So long as the lower echelons of the oligarchy administered the programmes at the county and community levels, they insisted upon being given authority to use discretion in their activities these included impressing on Negroes that they had no rights. There were privileges that a Negro might enjoy, but these men and women in the local offices were free to decide if he was the 'right kind of nigger' to merit them. The following scene describes the interplay of sentiments, the caricature of aid to the needy, the straining through local prejudices, as two stereotypes confront each other.

'An elderly Negro woman was visiting before the fire on the hearth of her simple cottage when an automobile was heard braking with great noise outside. The old woman excused herself . . . "Wait a minute, I'll be back," she said.

'Through the open door, as she stepped on the porch, an automobile could be seen with three young white girls straining with expectant faces from the rear seat.

'A young white man hoisted a cardboard carton to his shoulder and came towards the house.

'"Good Morning," the old woman called to him.

'"Good Morning, Aunty," the man replied as he set the box on the edge of the porch, "I brought your rations to you, Aunty, because I knew you didn't have any way to get to town to get them, and I know you need them."

'"Oh, Mr Roosevelt, you too good to me. You sure takes care of me, Mr Roosevelt," the old woman said in tones dripping gratitude.

'The girls in the car giggled.

'The man with a rather unconvincing air of authority and

in a not quite commanding voice went on, "You got your slip to see the doctor, ain't you?"

' "Yes sir, yes sir, I got it just like you give it to me, Mr Roosevelt," his relief client assured him.

' "All right then. Now your appointment to see the doctor is for next Tuesday. You tell that old nigger up the road that got the wagon to see you get to town so you can see the doctor at 9.30. Tell him if he don't bring you to town he needn't come to me looking for nothing. If he don't bring you to town he can't get no more relief."

' "He bring me, Mr Roosevelt, he sure to bring me. You know he going to do what you say. Everybody do what you say."

' The girls in the car were still giggling.

' The relief worker turned to go and called back, "All right Aunty, you come by to see me when you come to the doctor, Tuesday."

' "I sure will, Mr Roosevelt. God bless you, Mr Roosevelt, don't know what poor widow women would do without you, Mr Roosevelt."

' As the car moved off the girls broke into laughter.

' The old woman dragged her box inside. She opened the door of a cupboard beside her fireplace and began placing the groceries brought to her on its shelves. As she did so she commented to her visitor, "Roosevelt, I know he ain't no Roosevelt. You have to humour these peckerwoods to get along here in this country. You know sometimes he come out here three times a week to get something to laugh about. I'll tell you something: I feed half of this community out of this closet." '

The 'Old Nigger' and the 'peckerwood' had met and sought what satisfaction each could get by playing out stereotyped roles.

The South expected respect for stereotyped patterns of behaviour. Every white man, whatever his status, must be respected as wielding power. Every Negro must recognize that power from which there was no appeal. Every Negro must concede his helplessness, his defencelessness, and his being a little

or very stupid. As Negroes claimed the benefits of the New Deal
agencies, they were called on to show the small fry of the oligarchy, who themselves were enjoying white collar relief by
being given jobs dispensing blue collar or collarless relief, that
their 'attitudes were right'. The right attitude included obeying
the etiquette prescribed. According to the etiquette the Negro's
turn in the agency offices came after all whites had been served;
the Negro presented his claim in the pose of the supplicant; he
accepted the decision of the representatives of the agency without question; he might return another day to appeal against an
unfavourable decision, if he presented his appeal as an expression
of his own stupidity or incomprehension, and never as a challenge to the rightness or wisdom of the previous decision.

In the small town and rural areas, the cake of custom remained
unyielding in many things and the hand of the authority of the
oligarchy remained heavy. Larger and larger numbers of Negroes
left such areas and found homes and jobs in the cities. In the
cities Negroes found better opportunities for action to improve
their status, and more freedom to challenge the absolutism of
the oligarchy.

A number of things happened to Negroes in this period to
give them a sense of pride and worth. New achievements in-
spired them to greater efforts in their own behalf. Slum clearance
projects in Southern cities became monuments to Negroes of
Distinction—the J. C. Napier Homes in Nashville, the John
Hope Homes in Atlanta, the Charles H. Johnson Homes in
Bristol, Virginia, and many more. The Victory Ships of World
War II were named after famous Americans and included the
uss *Booker T. Washington* and the uss *Frederick Douglass*.
While distinguished Negroes of the past were being honoured,
deserving Negroes of the present achieved positions of distinc-
tion. Dr Ralph Bunche, Mrs Edith Sampson, Dr E. Franklin
Frazier, Dr Channing Tobias, Dr Charles S. Johnson, and Rev.
Archibald Carey held United Nation posts. New York,
Chicago, and Detroit elected Negroes to the U.S. Congress.
Judge William H. Hastie, Judge Irving C. Mollison, and Judge
Herman E. Moore were appointed to federal judgeships. Out-
side of the South in a dozen cities, Negroes held judgeships;
they sat in sixteen state legislatures. Within the South they were

elected to city councils in Tennessee, Kentucky, North Carolina, and Virginia and became members of boards of education in Knoxville, Tennessee, Atlanta, Georgia, and Raleigh, North Carolina. The Negro's role in American political life was not yet a representative one, but it was a sturdy new growth that had taken root since 1930.

None of these things happened through the good offices of the Southern Oligarchy. The executive and judicial branches of the federal government and a growing Negro electorate had used their powers to make them possible. President Roosevelt and President Truman used more than their appointive powers to advance the Negro's cause over the protest of the oligarchy. On June 25, 1941, President Roosevelt issued Executive Order 8802, ordering that there should be no discrimination in employment in defence industries or the government, and proceeded to establish a federal Fair Employment Practices Committee to effect compliance with his order. The Selective Service Act of 1940 removed discriminations in drafting and training men for the armed forces of the United States. In the course of World War II, the following numbers of Negroes served:

$$\begin{array}{rl} \text{Army} - & 700,000 \\ \text{Navy} - & 165,000 \\ \text{Coast Guard} - & 5,000 \\ \text{Marine Corps} - & 17,000 \end{array}$$

All avenues to officer commissions in the several services were opened to Negroes, including West Point and Annapolis. Colonel B. O. Davis, Sr., top-ranking Negro officer in the army when World War II came, did not meet the fate that Colonel Young had known in World War I. Colonel Davis became the first Negro general officer in the United States Army. When World War II was over, the armed services by presidential direction proceeded towards desegregation in their ranks, and at all of their installations.

On December 5, 1946, President Truman issued Executive Order 9708, creating a federal Committee on Civil Rights. When the Committee had reported, the President sent a message on civil rights to Congress in February, 1948, Mr Truman forthrightly stated his position. It was not one to win friends among the oligarchy on whom he correctly calculated his political fortune did not depend.

'We believe that all men are created equal and that they have the right to equal justice under the law.

'We believe that all men have the right to freedom of thought and of expression and the right to worship as they please.

'We believe that all men are entitled to equal opportunities for jobs, for homes, for good health and for education.

'We believe that all men shall have a voice in their government and government should protect, not usurp, the rights of the people.

'These are the basic civil rights which are the source and the support of our democracy.

'We shall not, however, finally achieve the ideals for which this nation was founded so long as any American suffers discrimination as a result of his race, or religion, or colour, or the land of origin of his forefathers.

'The protection of civil rights begins with the mutual respect for the rights of others which all of us should practise in our daily lives.

'The protection of civil rights is the duty of every government which derives its powers from the consent of the people.

'The federal Government has a clear duty to see that constitutional guarantees of individual liberties and of equal protection under the laws are not denied or abridged anywhere in our Union. That duty is shared by all three branches of the Government, but it can be fulfilled only if the Congress enacts modern comprehensive civil rights laws, adequate to the needs of the day, and demonstrating our continuing faith in the free way of life.

'Legislation Recommended:

'I recommend, therefore, that the Congress enact legislation at this session directed towards the following specific objectives:

(1) Establishing a permanent Commission on Civil Rights,

a Joint Congressional Committee on Civil Rights, and a Civil Rights Division in the Department of Justice.

(2) Strengthening existing civil rights statutes.

(3) Providing Federal protection against lynching.

(4) Protecting more adequately the right to vote.

(5) Establishing a Fair Employment Practice Commission to prevent unfair discrimination in employment.

(6) Prohibiting discrimination in interstate transportation facilities.

(7) Providing home rule and suffrage in Presidential elections for the residents of the District of Columbia.

(8) Providing statehood for Hawaii and Alaska and a greater measure of self-government for our island possessions.

(9) Equalizing the opportunities for residents of the United States to become naturalized citizens.

(10) Settling the evacuations claims of Japanese-Americans.'

In concluding his message, the President said:

'If we wish to inspire the peoples of the world whose freedom is in jeopardy, if we wish to restore hope to those who have already lost their civil liberties, if we wish to fulfil the promise that is ours, we must correct the remaining imperfections in our practice of democracy.'

The oligarchy saw this as an outright threat that it could not ignore. Suffering from delusions of power, its leaders set about to deny Harry S. Truman's return to the Presidency by organizing a 'States' Rights Party' with J. Strom Thurmond of South Carolina as candidate for President. Some Southern states, Alabama for example, refused to place Mr Truman's name on the ballot in 1948. Thurmond received 1,169,021 popular votes and six of the solid South states gave him thirty-nine electoral votes. The extremists in the oligarchy had 'shot their bolt'; the myth of its being an essential element of the Democratic Party was shattered.

CHAPTER V

Since 1950: Struggle for Survival

THE political misadventure of 1948 failed to chasten the oligarchy, which refused to be convinced that the tide of history was running against its kind and all that it stood for. In the next presidential election, in 1952, the Democratic Party faced the division between its liberal and conservative wings, and sought to satisfy both by choosing Adlai E. Stevenson, Governor of Illinois, as the presidential candidate and John Sparkman, Senator from Alabama, as the vice-presidential candidate. The campaign of these two candidates failed to mollify the oligarchy. Governor Stevenson expressed his liberal convictions in beautiful language and highly intellectual terms that made no comforting appeal to Southern voters. Senator Sparkman could not alter the vision Southerners formed of a Stevenson administration. In 1956, Senator Estes Kefauver of Tennessee, who was vice-presidential candidate with Governor Stevenson, had less appeal to the conservative Southern vote than Sparkman had four years before. The Republican candidates, Dwight D. Eisenhower and Richard M. Nixon, carried Florida, Tennessee, Texas and Virginia in both campaigns and added Louisiana to these in 1956.

The Republican administration that took control of the federal government with the support of some elements of the oligarchy in 1952, soon showed that these elements had purchased neither comfort nor respite with their votes for Eisenhower and Nixon. President Eisenhower authorized the United States Attorney General to represent the policy of the administration as opposed to school segregation, by entering a plea before the Supreme Court of the United States in the hearings that led to the 1954 decision on segregated public schools. Following the

1955 Supreme Court decision that authorized federal courts in the South to enforce compliance with its decision against segregated schools, President Eisenhower reminded the South that progress in school desegregation was expected. Despite the fact that President Eisenhower made no strong statement of his convictions about segregation, he insisted that the laws be respected. In 1957 he ordered federal troops into Arkansas, when the state authority failed to protect Negro children who had been admitted to the first school to be desegregated in Little Rock.

The judicial branch of the federal government, in a succession of decisions by the Supreme Court, has whittled away the legal basis of the oligarchy, to leave it outside the law, vociferously damning the high court. Among many decisions in the same spirit, the following have been selected by President L. H. Foster of Tuskegee Institute for his *Annual Race Relations Report for 1954*, to illustrate the legal definition of the status of the Negro in the United States.

'Since 1935 a series of decisions by the Supreme Court has assessed the validity of laws specifying the Negro's prerogatives and privileges. The following decisions emphasized the equality provision in circumstances of separation:

1. 1935—*Norris vs. Alabama*, against systematic exclusion of Negroes from juries.

2. 1938—*Gaines vs. Canada*, for provision of equal advantages in higher education.

3. 1941—*Mitchell vs. U.S.*, against *unlawful and unjust* discrimination in transportation and common carriers.

4. 1944—*Smith vs. Allwright*, against denying the Negro the opportunity to vote in primary elections.

5. 1950—*Brotherhood of Railroad Trainmen vs. Howard*, constraining labour organizations barring Negro membership, to safeguard Negroes' interest in collective bargaining.

'The following decisions have negated in some measure the principles of separation:

1. 1946—*Morgan vs. Virginia*, against segregation in interstate travel.

2. 1948—*Shelly vs. Kraemer* and *Hurd vs. Hodge,* against restrictive covenants which prescribed residential areas.

3. 1950—*Sweatt vs. Painter,* for admission of Negroes to the school with superior advantage when unequal provisions are made for higher education.

4. 1954—*Brown vs. Board of Education,* against separate educational facilities which are inherently unequal.

'The decision of May 17, 1954 as a reversal of the *Plessy vs. Ferguson* decision states a principle which rejects prescriptive and proscriptive laws, which specify application to Negroes. Significant for race relations is the fact that the new principle is one which is permissive in that it allows the individual freedom to work out race relations rather than legally denying or restricting freedom in their being worked out.'

All of these happenings left the oligarchy faced with some accomplished acts, from which it could see no turning back; but its determination to stem the tide was strengthened. In the hard core of control of oligarchy, state legislatures undertook to negate the Supreme Court decisions. These are some of the legislative actions taken:

1. Alabama, North Carolina, and Louisiana legislatures passed bills giving local school authorities the right to assign pupils to schools.

2. Alabama legislature passed a local bill permitting a county board of education to cancel the contracts of any teacher who favoured school integration or belonged to an organization advocating desegregation.

3. Alabama legislature passed a bill requiring a licence fee for NAACP solicitors.

4. Arkansas state senate blocked passage of a bill, approved by the lower house, to preserve school segregation.

5. Florida legislature passed a bill giving local school authorities the final authority in desegregating schools.

6. Georgia legislature made the expenditure of tax money for desegregated public schools by public school officials a felony.

7. Georgia, Louisiana, and South Carolina legislatures

authorized employment of lawyers to fight desegregation suits.

8. Louisiana legislature forbade the state board of education from approving integrated schools and forbade state colleges to recognize certificates of graduation from such schools.

9. Louisiana and Mississippi legal and educational advisory committees of the legislatures met jointly to exchange methods and ideas to preserve segregation.

10. Mississippi legislature authorized use of police power to maintain segregated schools.

11. Mississippi legislature passed a law providing fines and jail sentences for whites who might attend state-supported schools for Negroes.

12. South Carolina legislature voted to deny financial aid to any public school that desegregated.

The members of the oligarchy, who seek to cover their machinations under the claim of defending 'Constitutional Rights' in such legislation as that above, ignore Article VI, Clause 2 of the United States Constitution which reads: 'This Constitution and the laws of the United States . . . shall be the supreme law of the land . . . Anything in the Constitution or laws of any State to the contrary not-withstanding.'

The 85th Congress was organized in January, 1957 by the Democrats with members of the oligarchy occupying strategic posts, but they found their dominance challenged by Northern Democrats and some Republicans. They were faced with a Northern Democratic move to change the rules of the Senate, so as to take away that parliamentary device, the filibuster, that so often in the past had been used by the wilful Southern minority to obstruct the will of the majority. Despite encouragement by Vice President Richard M. Nixon, not enough Senators would support this change in the rules. The Republican administration introduced civil rights legislation which plagued the oligarchy. Representatives of the oligarchy fought the bill vigorously and succeeded in emasculating it, but the passage of any civil rights bill was for them a major defeat. The warning to them was clear: the Congres could, and perhaps would, make explicit and implicit guarantees of citizenship rights, regardless of the state boundaries within which a person lived.

The oligarchy seems to have gone beserk as the Supreme Court of the United States held to its decision on desegregation of schools. State legislatures went on a law-making rampage. On September 12, 1958, the Governor of Arkansas signed thirteen acts of the state legislature having to do with segregation and made them operative laws of that state. In 1960, the legislature of the state of Louisiana enacted legislation that obviously the Supreme Court would, and in short order did, declare unconstitutional.

Included among the new 'laws' passed by the Arkansas legislature there was one, to cover the 'crime of barratry', that was so written as to discourage legal assistance to plaintiffs from the National Association for the Advancement of Coloured People or the American Civil Liberties Union. The object of this legislation, and that like it in other Southern states was to leave the local citizen, with his limited financial resources and scarce local legal counsel, to provide the high cost of extensive court action and face the legal counsel paid by the state, which could use public funds to defray court costs.

The National Association for the Advancement of Coloured People has for decades carried on the legal fight for the civil rights of Negroes. Thurgood Marshall, the chief legal counsel for the NAACP, came to be the lawyer whom legal counsel of the oligarchy wanted least to meet in any court. All manner of discriminatory laws made by states and municipalities had been declared untenable by the higher courts when challenged by Mr Marshall and associated legal counsel. The Constitutional grounds upon which Mr Marshall made his cases was such that, in the decade of the 1950's, the Civil Rights Division of the Department of Justice of the United States entered more and more litigation on his side of the court contests.

Another 'law' in the Arkansas package was one to '*Require Affidavits from Administrators and Professional Employees Including Superintendents, Principals, and Instructors of the Elementary and Secondary Schools, and Colleges and Universities of the State of Arkansas Relative to all Incorporated and/or Unincorporated Associations and Organizations to which they have Belonged or Have Been Affiliated with for the Past Five Years; to Provide Penalties for Failure to Comply and Other Purposes.'* If this law was used in Arkansas as laws like it were already being used in other Southern states, members of the NAACP, or other organizations that advocated non-segregation, would face dismissal from their jobs and be subjected to punitive treatment by the political and financial powers of the communities in which they lived.

In 1961, there is still demand from some quarters for more civil rights legislation by the national Congress. The difficulty in getting such legislation enacted in this body, where the oligarchy is strong, and usually has the support of non-Southern conservative Republicans, discourages undertaking enactment of laws in this area. There is argument by others that legislation is already sufficient, that interpretation of the laws by the courts is clear enough and that the need is for forthright enforcement of the laws by the executive branch of the United States government. This enforcement appears to be a commitment by President John F. Kennedy and his brother, Attorney General Robert Kennedy. In the first six months of the Kennedy administration, determined enforcement of the laws of the United States has been undertaken.

Whatever laws are in force, and whatever machinery there is for their enforcement, can apply only when the people themselves take advantage of them. The oligarchy can ignore court decisions and continue to enforce its 'laws', unless the people challenge their application. During the 1950's, Negroes all over the South began making use of their legal prerogatives. The most widely publicized action was the boycott of segregated buses in Montgomery, Alabama. The successful desegregation of public transportation in that city effectively established 'non-violent protest' as a social instrument of Negroes seeking unrestricted participation in the social life of the United States. As spokesman for the Negroes of Montgomery, the Reverend Martin Luther King, Jr. became a national leader, whose philosophy came to be expressed in the action of Negroes throughout the South.

On February 1, 1960, college students in Greensboro, North Carolina entered a store and sat at a segregated lunch counter.

A report by the Southern Regional Council listed sixty-five Southern cities to which this practice had spread in two months, to become known as the 'sit-in movement'. In many places in the South students were arrested by policemen and attacked by mobs, but their persistence, despite being jailed and 'roughed-up', brought about desegregation in many parts of the South. The 'sit-ins' were followed by students standing in lines before theatres that segregated patrons, students visiting churches in which Negro worshippers were not welcome, and students going on beaches from which Negroes had been excluded. The 'stand-ins', 'kneel-ins', 'wade-ins' further expressed the determination of students to bring about desegregation. In the spring of 1961, groups of white and Negro passengers began using transportation facilities on a non-segregated basis and came to be known as 'Freedom Riders'. In each attack on an aspect of segregation the experience of the challengers was the same: threats and attacks by mobs, arrests by the police, and jailings.

The oligarchy, through its police force and the local courts, sought to enforce its 'laws', regardless of the construction placed on these specious legalisms by the federal courts.

The decade of the 1960's has begun with the oligarchy and mobs allied against federal authority, southern Negroes, and Americans outside of the South who show a growing determination that the oligarchy's will shall no longer be done.

PART II

Disadvantage to the Many
Sociological Perspective

Disadvantage to the Many—

Statistics, colourless figures, tell a story of a people's quality to those who can read behind the digit and the decimal. There are abundant statistics of the South in the censuses, and in a variety of reports that count people and arrange them in categories. The South also has a literature that describes its people and places. Both figures and words present the same picture: too many impoverished people, too many untaught people, too many people whose well-being is disregarded, too many people for whom places of disadvantage are maintained. Decade follows decade and in the record of each, Southern people remain below the national level comparing unfavourably with people who live in other regions.

The disadvantages of the many in the South are the obverse of the social coin that gives power to the few. The pattern of social life, with the powerful few and powerless many, the few wealthy and the many poor, is defended as being a democratic society. The network of the oligarchy covers the southern region, with its representatives in the small towns and by-ways, where they arrogantly assert their roles of dominance.

Day in and day out, in the ordinary affairs of life in any community, members of the oligarchy declare their power. In one area the assertion of power came in a minor controversy over a simple drain across a roadway. A young engineer fresh out of college eagerly approached this first task on his first job. This task, with top priority, was waiting for him. He drove the truck with the metal pipe and four Negro labourers to the spot where the pipe was to be put under the road. Then he set the labourers to digging the trench in which it would be laid.

An old man sauntered up, took a look at the drain, and barked out; 'Take it back; it's too little.'

The engineer pushed his new pith helmet back on his head and looked this meddler over, from his sweat-stained old felt hat to his muddy brogans, before replying as he felt a public official should.

67

'Listen, old man,' he told the dissatisfied citizen, 'that's what the County sent you and that's what you're gonna get.'

The old man contemptuously squirted tobacco juice at the pipe, squinted at the engineer and told him, 'Hell, boy, you talking to the County now.' He wasn't boasting. He was the owner of the land stretching for fifteen miles on either side of the road. His opinions were respected as instructions by the office holders in that county.

The oligarchy rules from the farming community to the County seat, from the industrial city to the State Capitol. This rule is significant because of what it does to people. In its exercise of power, the Southern oligarchy has done and is doing to the South, and to the rest of the nation, something that causes Americans all over the land to pay out to those who rule the South.

Basically, this power structure is not different from others. It is concerned with maintaining itself; that objective is its first concern. To be sustained it requires an economic base that supports its political structure. To function efficiently it requires a social organization that re-enforces it. For a stable economy and an orderly society after its preferred pattern, the oligarchy requires an ideology and emotion-stirring rituals for the people it controls. The thought-pattern it fosters is not acceptance of time-served folk beliefs. Rather it is a systematic compound of myth, rationale, beliefs, fostered fears, and nourished hopes. An elaborate orthodoxy supports the oligarchy's power to punish deviation and to reward loyalty. For the truly faithful, guilt feeling or a sense of gratification are sufficient punishment or reward.

The result is a social structure within which the oligarchy enjoys power as a sectarian core, fanatical in its zeal for the cause. Its unwavering dedication has served to give the nation grievous economic problems and painful political misfortunes.

CHAPTER VI

The Mecca and the Sainted

The SOUTH as an ideology is America's tragedy; a tragedy of heroic proportions difficult to comprehend, played-out across a century of American life; compounded of much suffering, generation after generation, involved with the self-pity of the sufferers and the brutality of the provocateurs; the accounts of its course and dramatic scenes incite to partisanship and bring about confusion.

THE SOUTHERNER is not just a person who lives in a specific region of the United States. He uncovers before the statue of Jefferson Davis at Montgomery, and on the portico of the State Capitol, there bows reverently over the bronze star embedded in the floor, to mark the spot where Davis took the oath of office as 'President of the Confederate States of America'. He celebrates Decoration Day and the birthdays of Robert E. Lee and Nathan Bedford Forrest. On these holidays he hoists the flag of the short-lived Confederacy. He has reservations about 'one nation indivisible' for which the stars and stripes wave. He is not a Southerner; he prides himself on being THE SOUTHERNER.

THE SOUTHERNER is an identification assumed by people to whom it bears peculiar, exclusive meaning. They define the meaning to suit themselves. These people, conceiving themselves to be an elite, exclude from the identification much of the population of the Southern states. They employ their own dogma and mythology to manipulate the people around them for their own satisfaction. As they use the term, SOLID SOUTH, it refers to a tightly knit elite that has arrogated power to itself. To understand what America has suffered from the SOLID SOUTH, and what people who live in the Southern states have suffered, it is necessary to put the SOLID SOUTH in sharpest focus.

Events or incidents that suggest change or reveal a lack of solidarity in THE SOUTH are awe-inspiring to the elite—the ruling oligarchy. Such events should awe those who see in them omens presaging doom. One of these events can strike them with terror and provoke them to frenzy. Any decisive incident must be denied in hysterical clamour. The South is solid! The SOLID SOUTH will never accept deviations from its old ways! The oligarchy can't suffer the belief that the SOLID SOUTH is going, really going.

THE SOUTHERNER is fanatically committed to an ideology designed to preserve the SOLID SOUTH. The ideology, stripped of double-talk, is simple. Its doctrine is white supremacy—control of the economy and the government by white men, some white men. It limits ' white ' to mean those who share its beliefs and condone its methods of acquiring and maintaining power. To carry out its purposes, it demands freedom from constraint. The constraining influences of religion, of ethical beliefs, of a political creed are rejected. The only constraints it respects are those imposed by its singular faith. Somehow it is mystically empowered to impose constraints on religion, on morality, and on political creeds. The ideology demands constraining power.

Myths that re-enforce the ideology and make imperative propagation of its doctrine are strongly charged with emotion. In thousands of village, town and city court-house squares stand memorials to the Confederate dead, reminders of past injury and obligation to avenge it. On occasion the old Confederate flag flutters above the little stone man. The pedestal on which he stands carries the graven wail:

> *No Nation rose so free from guilt;*
> *No Nation fell so free from stain.*

THE SOUTH has its mecca, its shrines, its sainted, and its holy days.

This ideology gives THE SOUTHERNER a distinctive place among Americans. It makes him the notable subverter all over the United States. THE SOUTHERNERS are not simply different in inconsequential characteristics, such as speech, habits, and personality. Their ideology gives them a mission. This mission is to subvert American institutions.

Like other subversive minorities, THE SOUTHERNERS dislike being identified as such. They insist that they are people of a faith that deserves and claims the protection of the authority they would destroy. THE SOUTHERNERS are especially vulnerable in this effrontery since it is a historical fact that they have attempted to overthrow the government of the United States by force of arms. They refuse to deny that they reject the principles and practices of democratic government. They have been consistent in holding our democratic institutions in contempt and in boldly defying the federal authority. They do not accept the democratic creed and they show abhorrence for democratic ways.

To begin with they reject the proposition that democracy rests on universal suffrage. Those who do not share their faith are considered to be unfit to share in the processes of government. They must be ruled by THE SOUTHERNERS, who are morally obliged to make laws to keep them from voting, and when legal deterrents fail, to employ intimidation and violence.

THE SOUTHERN ideology insists not only on subversion in domestic affairs; it injects its influences in international relations. A world power with an ideology comparable with that of THE SOUTH was Nazi Germany; a similar ideology may be found today in the Union of South Africa.

Each generation since 1865 has announced a 'New South' and applauded some newness so long as the old contours were not altered and THE SOUTH's integrity was preserved. There has been no objection to the new so long as it was not different from the old. These many new Souths never encouraged free communication, co-operation, fraternization. There simply could be no new South that was different, so long as each new generation cherished the foibles and fancies of tradition and patterned its behaviour on that of a bygone era. Moulded in reverence for the past, the thoughtful and the prayerful could seldom in maturity unshackle themselves. Now something new, but also different, threatens to come to the South through its schools.

Already their young have been turned against them. The armed services, in which every able-bodied young man must have a tour of duty, are already desegregated. In those two years of military training, young men are indoctrinated with a philosophy of no-prejudice and no-discrimination. The young men from the South have accepted this order of things. If the schools follow the pattern and have the influence of the armed services, THE SOUTHERNER may have no heir to carry on.

THE SOUTHERNERS, as champions of States' rights, enjoy the company of fellow-travellers. On the States' rights rostrum, the would-be exploiters of the nation's reserves of natural resources join the would-be exploiters of the nation's reserves of human resources. THE SOUTHERNERS as a subversive minority have survived owing to the support that they have received from special interest allies. The tide-lands oil interests, the natural gas interests, the electrical power interests, the timber and grass-lands interests ally themselves to the cheap-labour interests in a spirited revival, spreading the gospel of States' rights. The old testament of nullification has become John C. Calhoun's epistle on interposition. THE SOUTHERNERS have the support of other protectionists, which is a negation of the principles of free enter-prise and free competition.

A subversive minority requires a 'whipping boy' against which antagonism is directed to close its ranks. THE NEGRO has been THE SOUTH's obvious whipping boy, an admirable whipping boy. His easy visibility prevents mistakes. His colour and his poverty make him readily recognizable. Negro South-erners and white Southerners may have common bonds of understanding and sympathy that make for strong sentimental attachments, but THE NEGRO is something else, a useful beast of burden not to be admitted to human fellowship.

While THE NEGRO is a convenient whipping boy he presents some difficulty in that role because he may not be labelled subversive. THE NEGRO is a *disadvantaged minority* with an utterly simple philosophy and no ideology. That philosophy is summed up as 'me-tooism'. All of his efforts are directed to-wards getting included in. In *where* doesn't seem important: in anywhere and everywhere—in the congregation or in the gang;

in the labour union or in the Kiwanis; in the beer-joint or in the school. Whatever America offers, THE NEGRO wants part of it. THE SOUTHERNERS can unify their ranks for concerted action if that action directly or indirectly is avowed to keep THE NEGRO out.

THE SOUTHERNERS plead plaintively to be left alone in dealing with this species that they domesticated and made useful. They argue that they alone know him; they alone can harness him in continued usefulness. They justify all of their strange actions, foolish and subversive, on the grounds that these are essential to control THE NEGRO, who threatens their institutions, their racial purity, their very existence.

The Southerner is not content to be contained in his preempted province. Commanding officers of training centres during World War II were bound to enforce an order from General George C. Marshall which, in essence, required troops in training to respect the customs of the people among whom their camps were located. SOUTHERNERS welcomed this order as their victory. Outside the South the situation was different. Army officers who were disciplined members of the SOUTHERN conspiracy behaved as if its claims upon them took precedence over military discipline. In some cases special orders were required to remind these officers that 'respect for local customs' was not a concession applicable only in the South. They had to be told that they could no more put up 'For White Only' signs in Massachusetts than other officers could take such signs down in Virginia. As is the case with all subversive zealots they never doubted the rightness of their cause and resented any restraints imposed on its furtherance.

The frayed old banner with its faded stars and bars, too rent and tattered to wave, trembles over shouting voices and stamping feet. The nation's oldest subversive minority mobilizes its forces for a costly rear-guard action. If its delaying and harassing tactics can stay a decisive conclusion THE SOUTH may again take the offensive. Its provocateurs are inciting to riot. Its logicians are using its dialectics to challenge the nation's unchallengeable institutions.

At Montgomery, 'The Mecca', and in the hinterland of the rest of Alabama, more simply outrageous actions of the oli-

c*

garchy have occurred in the past decade than have taken place in any other area of the South.

When Autherine Lucy, the first Negro student to be admitted to the University of Alabama, was driven from the campus, the only case of successful mob violence at an institution of higher learning in the South occurred.

In Birmingham, a harmless feeble-minded Negro, who was not even accused of any offence to anyone, was taken from a street by men, reputed to be Ku Klux Klansmen, who performed a crude operation of emasculation on him. The fiends who perpetrated this act had some twisted notion that they were serving notice on Negroes of what they could expect if they did not 'stay in their places'.

The Negro leader who has shown the greatest courage in Alabama is the Reverend Fred L. Shuttlesworth of Birmingham. Because he led the fight for desegregation the church he pastors has been bombed twice; the parsonage in which his family slept was destroyed by bombs; he has been beaten by a mob in open daylight on the street; he has been arrested, jailed and judged guilty in local courts of violating ordinances of the city government.

At the city of Anniston a bus carrying 'Freedom Riders' was burned by a mob.

At Tuskegee, the town in which the famous Tuskegee Institute is located, the four-sided city boundaries were re-drawn by an act of the legislature into a crazy twenty-six-sided shape in order to put all Negroes who had become registered voters outside of the corporation. After four years of litigation in the courts, the Supreme Court ordered the original boundaries restored and the state legislature then appointed a special committee to consider plans for the abolition of the county by dismembering it and attaching parts of it to several adjoining counties.

In Montgomery, hoodlums with clubs terrorized Negroes on the streets, while policemen looked on without interfering. When Negroes gathered in a church to march to the State Capitol building for a prayer service, the policemen who gathered to prevent them from marching took no action against a white mob that had gathered outside the church.

When students of the Alabama State Teachers College in Montgomery demonstrated against segregation in public buildings, the Governor of the state demanded that they be expelled. Before a television audience he lolled arrogantly in his chair while the president, who had been head of the college for thirty-five years, stood humiliated before him to report that his demands had been carried out. The most distinguished member of the faculty of this college, Professor Lawrence D. Reddick, was dismissed by the Governor because he had appeared in New York City several years before, on a programme on which the Russian diplomat Vishinsky also spoke.

When the Freedom Riders appeared in Montgomery in the summer of 1961, a mob awaited them at the bus depot and attacked and beat members of the group without police interference. The failure of police officials of the state of Alabama or of Montgomery to maintain order caused Attorney General Robert Kennedy to order United States Marshals into the city so to do.

As Attorney General of the State from 1955 to 1959, and Governor since 1959, John Patterson, has taken his position as the champion of States' rights and defender of the faith of segregation. He has shown his determination to uphold ' our laws ', meaning the laws of the state of Alabama that have been declared unconstitutional by the federal courts. The mobs that have gathered from time to time have not been regarded as a menace to the peace of the community, while unarmed Negroes making non-violent protest have been considered a menace to the public welfare.

Nowhere else has the oligarchy taken its stand as unashamedly as in Montgomery. There, no moderate has spoken out since Governor James E. Folsom left office in 1959. Through all of the violence that has exploded in the state, despite all of the malfeasance of public officials, and in view of a continuing display of contempt in the state for federal law punctuated by wildly seditious statements by public officials, neither of the two esteemed Senators, nor any of the members of the House of Representatives from Alabama in the United States Congress has reproved anyone there or taken a stand for the United States Constitution each has sworn to uphold.

Montgomery advertises itself as 'The Cradle of the Confederacy' and at its boundaries where the chief traffic artery, 'The Jefferson Davis Highway', enters the city, a sign carrying the figure of a robed horseman welcomes travellers in the name of the Ku Klux Klan.

CHAPTER VII

Psychological Warfare

'I feel that a large part of the success of public affairs depends on the newspaper men—not so much on the editorial writers, because we can live down what they say, as upon the news writers, because the news is the atmosphere of public affairs. Unless you get the right setting of affairs—disperse the right impression—things go wrong. . . .' WOODROW WILSON: *The First Presidential Press Conference, 15 March, 1913.*

THE state of political affairs in the South since 1876 has shown a dissident minority contained within another such minority in the nation itself. In 1876, Rutherford B. Hayes acquiesced to the return of the Southern oligarchy to power, after ten years of struggle between those loyal to the Union and those committed to the preservation of the cause of the Confederacy, notwithstanding military defeat. Not until events in the decade of the 1950's presaged the undoing of what the oligarchy had done upon its return to power, did the controversy between the Negro and the oligarchy, and the oligarchy and the nation reach a stage of bitter psychological warfare. Never before have two minorities in this country been so insistent upon having the attention of the nation. Each presses its claim to sympathy, soliciting the neutrality of those it may not convince to partisanship.

The blanketing assault on feeling and reason leaves no escape for those who would not concern themselves with this matter. Those who are interested, but uncommitted, struggle in confusion against tide and undertow of claim and counter-claim. From platform and pulpit, through press, radio, and television Americans are being bombarded with words—words that are intended to create the atmosphere in which this public affair is to be considered and decided.

To further their ends, the minorities—Southern oligarchy and Negro—must present themselves as they would be seen in the controversy, each creating images of itself as it never was. Equally important are the images of each by the other—as it knows the other never to have been. The oligarchy's image of itself as virtue outraged is not new; the Negro's image of it as malicious force outraging virtue are as old. The Negro's images of itself are new—a figure emerging out of the dormant cocoon in natural metamorphosis from its humbler past. The oligarchy's images of it are as new—a poisonous form, undreamed of, emerging from the long quiet of the chrysalis.

The cult of power, poised as threat or ruthlessly applied, has its own psychological appeal. The image is created of the strong as tender—until provoked to a shattering use of strength. The oligarchy describes itself as holding the leash on the brute strength of the Southern people. On occasion it will suggest the nightmare of havoc that would be wrought should it unleash this might, already armed with hatred and lethal weapons. This image is awesome enough to make many people dread the moment when Negroes and Northerners push the oligarchy beyond its endurance. They ask themselves, 'Is it not wisdom to halt short of this step of provocation?' To strike such fear to the hearts of men is power in all-out psychological warfare.

Another image the oligarchy creates is of itself as the taught and the able. Those of the oligarchy are learned and their competence, political and economic, has been demonstrated. Would anyone, whatever his sympathies, want the political wreckage and economic ruin that ignorant and incompetent Negroes would make of the South should they be given ill-advised responsibility? They point backward to the era of Reconstruction following the Civil War, both to justify the counter-revolution in which they wrested power, and to give an object lesson on what happens when the untaught and the unfit assume responsibility.

Those left cold by these images find the oligarchy reaching for their heart-strings, with an image of the tragic, beleaguered minority surrounded and left only the choice of honour. Until

the last decade emphasis was on numbers. Those who wrote on
the subject accepted in simple gullibility the Southern uneasiness
as a numerical minority surrounded by blacks. For two decades
now the census figures have controverted the psychological usefulness of this image. There is now a new formulation designed
to keep the advantage of sympathy for the underdog:

But the way we see it in the South, the way I see it, is that
the Negro is in a majority, because he has the country behind
him. He could have the support of the federal army.

Another image the oligarchy would offer of itself is that of
the unsullied—pure in heart, mind and body—who would suffer
contamination from educational, economic, and social intima-
cies with Negroes. Brothers of the blood everywhere are called
upon to stay this ominous threat that would dull the intellect,
lower the living standards, and mongrelize the stock of the
noble Anglo-Saxon. Other white people, the nation over, are
asked to imagine themselves so threatened and, when they have
finished shuddering at the prospect, to rally to the defence of the
oligarchy against it.

These in sum are the oligarchy's major images of itself. Should
others see it as it would have them do, its beachheads are won.
To get these images broadcast afar, it uses the device of charging those who see it differently with being prejudiced. This becomes a challenge to editors and working newsmen to temper the
obvious and qualify the facts so as to include the South's images
of itself in their reporting and commentary.

The South's images of the Negro require acquaintance with
the chameleon, for credence in the supposition that some human
beings too are constantly blending and shading their colours.
The reassuring foolish grin of the Negro in one view becomes a
horrible grimace in another light and a sinister leer seen from
a different angle.

The obsessive image of the Negro that the oligarchy is loath
to erase is that of the faithful, loyal 'Good Nigra'. This Negro
is satisfied with the state of things in the South. He is obedient.
Some Negro is usually to be found giving comfort to the
oligarchs by acting out this role. The Montgomery, Alabama

Advertiser found solace in a blown-up, front-page Sunday story reporting: 'Notasulga Negro Mass Meeting Hears Leader Back Segregation.' The group estimated at one hundred persons in the village of Notasulga, was reported as having been told by the unknown 'college president':

> 'You can't hurry God and you can't hurry a Southern white man and, just like from God, you can get anything you need and deserve from the white man, but you've got to ask him in the right manner.'

In every community there is some Negro who gives expression to this sentiment for the credulous outsider for whom a Southern oligarch arranges a confrontation.

In another image the Negro does not have this unshakeable loyalty. He is weak in will-power and gullible. Some enemy of the oligarchy is always leading him astray. He easily wanders in the wake of some Pied Piper to action that he really does not want or understand. He did this after the Civil War when seduced by Republican carpetbaggers into participation in government. He heeds the blandishments of the strangest confidence characters: the NAACP, the Republican Party, the United States Supreme Court, the President of the United States, and the Pope. A Negro occasionally is deluded by some subversive idea planted by one of these so as to require his friends of the oligarchy to do a little gentle convincing. The oligarchy gives assurance that it does not relax its vigilance to protect this lovable stupid creature from these malicious predators; that the Negro can be convinced to return from a wayward adventure if sometimes it is necessary to shoot him, burn him, beat him, starve him, or put him in jail.

There is the image of the culturally unassimilable Negro and the image of him as the incompetent and defective. There are fine points of western civilization that he cannot be taught. He is diseased, ignorant, and immoral. But, he learns fast enough to get 'uppity' and refuse the place the oligarchy has fashioned for him. Negroes provide the jewels of cooks, the tenderest nurse-maids, and the most indefatigable burden-bearers in spite of their defects.

A new image recently sketched for circulation by whites is that of the Negro who has made more progress than any other people in like circumstances in history. His southern neighbours take credit for this achievement by describing themselves as encouraging him and making his progress possible. Those who would be clever call for the incomplete data on the Negro's status to be used to describe his educational attainment and his economic status in 1960 as compared to earlier dates. They seek to avoid comparisons which show the persistence of differentials between whites and Negroes. The logical conclusion of this argument is that the pushing and striving Negro today is a sadly ungrateful example of foolish insatiability.

For many years Negroes were on the defensive. Apology, admitting limitation while ascribing it to lack of opportunity, was repeated time and time again. The Negro spent the energies of three generations after emancipation proving that the oligarch's images of him were caricatures. He accepted the challenge to defend himself. Every Negro of achievement bore the burden of the honour of a whole people. Every Negro miscreant bowed a whole people in shame. At long last came a generation of Negroes that decided there was an ample accumulation of evidence of mass achievement by Negroes. With this generation the Negro moved to the offensive as 'The New Negro', 'The Brown American'.

The faithful servitor, his indenture done, come to require his legitimate due, is the basic image the Negro has created of himself. He never ceases to remind America of his services, under trying conditions, in war and in work. America is not allowed to forget his martial services from the fall of Crispus Attucks with the first patriots on Boston Common to black boys in the freezing mud of Korea. Denial of support for his cause carries the shame of one warrior brother's ingratitude for the several services of the other brother's willing right arm.

A black skin covering all-American bone and sinew is another of the Negro's images of himself. He claims no memories, no ways, no tradition, no beliefs but those acquired in America. No hyphen links him to a past that might raise a suspicion of divided allegiance.

The good citizen accepting his responsibilities despite denial of his privileges is another image of himself the Negro has created. He has always been amenable to law however slow the pace of judicial procedure. He has made no laws unto himself. He sues for his due under the laws of his country asking that no *i* of that law be undotted nor any *t* uncrossed. It is a compelling image that asks neither mercy nor privilege—only simple justice.

The Negro's newest image of himself has come with the leadership of ministers in the desegregation movement in various parts of the South. In this image the Negro becomes the paragon of the non-violent Christian. He uses passive resistance. His weapons are Christian faith and Christian love against those who oppose him with power and guns and bombs.

These in sum are the Negro's images of himself. Should others see as he would have them do, his beachheads are won. To get these images broadcast afar, he uses the device of charging those who see it differently with being prejudiced. This is his challenge to editors and working newsmen.

The Negro's images of the oligarchy are incomplete, suggestive sketches. He takes care not to alienate white men who offer whatever degree of sympathy for his cause. The self-identified 'rebel' he recognizes as a rebel. These by their own admission of avowed intent to obstruct his advancement are the enemies of his cause. He readily admits their local power and their licence to exercise it. In doing so he looks to other white men, whose professed faith his enemies deny and whose power they challenge. He nimbly manœuvres so that the oligarchy presents itself to view in postures he need not describe. He invokes the law and leaves the oligarchy to declare its own outlawry. The oligarchy scourges him, he simply makes his scars visible. Somebody offers him a job. He takes it and lets the oligarchy prevent him from working. He stops riding the bus and lets the oligarchy dust off some obscure law to make him stop walking. He disappoints many by not offering images of the oligarchy. Why should he? Enough of the oligarchs set out caricatures of their kind upon any small provocation.

These then are the combatants. What are they fighting about? What objectives are attacked and defended? The oligarchy claims the enjoyment of privileges conferred on it by God and safeguarded by laws that it has made. It is determined to preserve these privileges against any who would remove them and to resist any attempt Negroes shall make to invade them. It is these privileges that are under attack. They include political preference, economic preference, educational preference, and preference in the enjoyment of the amenities and conveniences of modern civilization. Negroes make their attack on the grounds that these privileges are usurped rights. They want the oligarchy to continue to enjoy them as rights, sharing their enjoyment with Negroes by elimination of claim to preference. The oligarchy insists that it does not want them as rights stripped of preference, they are no good as rights, their worth lies in preferential enjoyment. Above all others, the oligarchy would defend as a right those discriminations it designed in its favour.

In their attack Negroes have used federal law as the fitting weapon for action to establish uniform rights. The oligarchy has responded with a counter-attack on federal law, as law. One of its objectives has become the negation of federal law by giving local legislation precedence over it. As to strategy, each of the combatants strives to maintain ramparts of legality about its position. Each has launched offensives to gain the moral support of the American people by expounding legal premises on which it stands.

The tactics of the opposing forces differ. The oligarchy, at some points of contact, is putting up stiff opposition; at others it seeks to delay or obstruct without giving battle; and at others it seeks to deflect attack by setting upon diversionary frays. The tactics of the Negro involve attack, attack, no let-up on the attack. Sometimes the attack is direct assault. At other points it is to set siege and carry on a battle of attrition. In some circumstances it feints, so as to trap the enemy forces into making depredations in ideological territory that incites stronger forces than its own to do battle.

States' Rights, Nullification, Interposition—all express a principle of political philosophy that may be used to lead through a tortuous labyrinth of argument. Serious-thinking Americans puzzle over these arguments. Their value in the current psycho-

logical war is that they are like two-edged swords. There are
admitted rights reserved for states and smaller local government
units that deserve protection. The oligarchy has a valid contention in principle. It would keep the argument at the level of
principle and by doing so gain acceptance of its cause. To
maintain this bulwark of legalism it assigns to the ramparts its
elite guard, those occupying high places in the Congress and in
state governments. This strategy is well planned. It carries the
prestige of high place, of proponents who are experts in government. It exploits the aura of history studded with gems of
oratory by the founding fathers of the nation. It is designed to
win men's minds, however reluctantly they may concede to
reasoning against their sentiments and moral convictions.

The Negro, aided by philosophical federalists on one flank
and by moralists on the other, makes a two-pronged counter-
attack. The argument of the federalists is that the founding
fathers of the nation did debate and fail to resolve this question. To get the original thirteen states into union they
deferred the decision on the boundary between federal and
state powers. The hope that subsequent fusion of interests would
reconcile this divergence failed to be realized. Rather, a pro-
gressive widening of the breach led to dissolution of the union
in rebellion by the States' rights adherents. The armed conflict
ended in the capitulation of the rebels. To settle this issue for
the future, an amendment to the Constitution was made specifying that rights reserved to the states were not to conflict with
those vested in the federal power. The other prong of this
counter attack, that spear-headed by the Negro's religious and
moral allies, makes the disclaimer that the affair in question
may not be considered in terms of application of this principle
at all. The principle was not formulated to cover a matter such
as this. They insist that this political principle was never
designed to abrogate morality or to provide for the mean and
petty schemes of unethical men.

The oligarchy's strategy faces Americans with the painful
dilemma of either supporting the Negro's claim to unrestricted
citizenship or supporting a profound political principle. The
Negro's strategy faces Americans with an equally grievous
dilemma, of supporting the oligarchy's political position or sup-

porting moral and religious values. The element of the people
that is expected to be convinced by reason finds itself under
terrific intellectual pressure.

The Negro leads his attack, to gain sentiments favourable to
his cause, by describing his status as 'second-class citizenship'
and by picturing that as being a loathsome position. No person
with human feelings would be relegated to or relegate another
to 'second-class citizenship'. All who can identify with Negroes
in this reject for them this disadvantage. It is in this manœuvre
that image creation becomes important. The Negro's images of
himself are those of a group that does not deserve the second-
class status. The oligarchy uses its images of the Negro in the
counter-attack with the claim that Negroes are a limited people
and can, in justice, enjoy only a limited citizenship. They would
invite other Americans to identify with them instead of with
Negroes. Calling for respect to be given to the blood tie, they imply
that those who identify with Negroes are stupid or otherwise
defective, morally perhaps, and may themselves be candidates
for second-class citizenship.

Another assault on the sentiments of the American people
comes in the Negro's appeal for sympathy by recital of the record
of atrocities committed against Negroes. Murders, bombings,
and other abuses are widely publicized. That these acts go unpunished is related to citizenship status and is used to alienate
the sympathy of some from the oligarchy's cause, even though
these do not necessarily sympathize deeply with the Negro. The
oligarchy would minimize these atrocities. A Mississippi poli-
tician sadly points out that, in 1955, only eight Negroes were
killed by whites and draws attention away from these by
reporting that eighteen Negroes were killed by Negroes, in the
same period.

The oligarchy would give the atrocity appeal a twist from
sympathy to fear. This twist takes the form of dire prediction
that the cup of the sympathetic will brim over when their sympathy shall have encouraged Negroes to foolhardy action that
will end in many more being killed. A bomb thrown here and
there is supposed to be greatly convincing. No arrests and no
fixing of responsibility are supposed to show the oligarchy to be
helpless in such circumstances.

The oligarchy seeks defections among those sympathetic to Negroes by showing their sweet reason in contrast to the Negro's utterly unreasonable behaviour. They enumerate the events that have marked the Negro's progress since slavery and describe how the tempo of granting the Negro privileges has been accelerated in the last two decades. In this attack, the spokesmen for some elements of the oligarchy are so reasonable as to accept the Negro's claims as entirely justified. They earnestly agree that these claims must be respected; the oligarchy itself honestly does respect them, they give assurance. The only threat to Negroes not having their claims satisfied is in the unreasonableness of the Negroes themselves. The Negro wants to have this satisfaction too fast and only on his own terms. The gradualists among the oligarchy seek to dissociate themselves from those of the oligarchy who emphatically assert that these claims will not now, or in the foreseeable future, be satisfied. The plea to 'just give us time—a little time' sounds reasonable enough to many people. Patience is a Christian virtue and Americans are disposed to respect those who have developed it as opposed to the impetuous. Negroes counter with the contention that ninety years is pretty gradual, and that ninety years of waiting shows the exercise of some little patience on their part.

In a charge from another point of the compass, the oligarchy describes the conflict as not being the making of the Negroes in the *South* where it has meaning. It is a malicious mischief on the part of Negroes and whites in the North. The major target in this attack is the National Association for the Advancement of Coloured People. This organization has been the agency for legal action by Negroes. It is charged that this organization first disturbs and then misleads Negroes in the South. Sentimental rejection of the provocateur is called for. Negroes counter with figures that adduce two-thirds of the NAACP membership to be Southern and ninety per cent of it to be Negro. The oligarchy seeks to have the organization placed on the Attorney General's subversive organizations list. Legislative action in the South would ban it as a legal organization and laws have been passed to penalize individuals who hold membership in it. State courts, presided over by members of the oligarchy have shamelessly joined in persecuting the NAACP. The attempt is made to alienate sympathy from the NAACP by describing it as a raiding party, swooping down out of the North to spread terror among Negroes and whites alike in a peaceful and contented South.

Another tactical manœuvre is that of the oligarchy to deploy raiding bands that hit widely scattered objectives thus keeping the Negro forces busy protecting occupied territory so as to preclude their making advances. This guerrilla activity behind the lines has been troublesome. As soon as one state law or municipal ordinance is declared untenable, others are enacted. The oligarchy boasts that this manœuvre will keep Negroes in the courts for a hundred years. Their aim is to maintain harrassment in territory which is virtually lost to them in the hope that a spirit of despair may be engendered. Moves in the state of Florida have been of this sort. Appearing before the Supreme Court in 1954, the Attorney General of that state accepted the principle of desegregation, advocated gradualism, and expressed the hope that integrated schools would come without too much trouble. One of Florida's Senators declared resistance to integration to be futile and reminded Floridians that it was going to be the law. The Superintendent of Public Instruction made implementation of the decision the responsibility of local school boards. After a period of temporizing, the Attorney General urged state legislation to block desegregation. No local school board integrated a school. The policy of the state government was revealed by the Governer thus: 'Reduced to simple terms our strategy has been to resist implementation in Florida by every lawful and peaceful means at our command.'

In the struggle at its fiercest, polite conventions are discarded and it becomes 'all-out' warfare. On the domestic front, the oligarchy marshalls its considerable power to prove that when organized it is a formidable adversary. As it puts other considerations aside and clears the deck for a 'no quarter given' engagement the threat becomes greater to the Negro's allies than it is to the Negro. Its organization in battle formation removes any doubt of the unity of the oligarchy as it stands boldly forth as 'the Oligarchy'. Such a decisive moment came when the '96' gave their ultimatum to the nation in 1956. The wording of the ultimatum had the merit of extending the debate, but the serious matter is the very fact of ultimatum.

The national administration, with many programmes that require the support of a Democratic Congress in which the oligarchy is powerful, faces difficult decisions in which the Negro's cause can become a significant factor. Among the perfidious ' 96 ' were some who can do the administration's programme damage. At that time the Chairman of the Agricultural Committee of the Senate, Allen J. Ellender of Louisiana was in a position to prevent President Eisenhower from getting a farm bill satisfactory to him. Senator Holland of Florida served notice that the Senate would take great care in approving Mr Eisenhower's nominees for federal Judgeships. Senator Eastland of Mississippi, Chairman of the Judiciary Committee of the Senate, fully appreciating his powers, needed to make no statement because he was a present danger with all frenetic warning lights blinking. The Eisenhower administration did support the case for desegregation before the Supreme Court and President Eisenhower's appointee to the Chief Justiceship was by way of becoming a Southern *bête noire* before Vice President Nixon claimed the desegregation decision to be a Republican achievement. President Kennedy, nearly a decade later, has to face the same Southern leaders in the Congress on the same issues.

The challenge is: allies of the Negro must be prepared to sacrifice the success of concerns vital to themselves if they support desegregation. Threats serve notice that these allies must withdraw the support they give to desegregation or they will suffer violence to interests of greater concern to them than desegregation is.

Individuals who show too great a zeal for desegregation must be prepared for sniping. Senator Herbert Lehman of New York was one of two Senators who expressed opposition to approval of Senator Eastland as Chairman of the Judiciary Committee. From Professor Raymond Moley in his column in *Newsweek* Mr Lehman gets a sneer and a swipe that should give comfort to the oligarchy. Writing about a bill before Congress sponsored by Senator Lehman, Professor Moley says:

'No more consecrated enemy of discrimination in the

South has ever raised his voice than Senator Herbert Lehman
of New York. For years he has demanded equal and identical
access to all services, public and private, for all citizens.'

'It is strange, therefore, to find him introducing a bill which
would make second-class economic citizens of hundreds of
thousands of people in New York and neighbouring states . . .'

After this gratuity, Professor Moley goes through a discussion
of preferences to be given different classes of users of electric
power developed with public funds.

Senator Lehman's problem was one that faces many Northern
Democrats. Regardless of whether they have been foremost in
the advancement of the Negro's cause from conviction or for
reasons of expediency, they have been advocates. Since 1936 the
Negro vote has been in their favour. The oligarchy is in a position to take reprisals and inflict damage on them and on the
Democratic Party. The efforts of the '96' gave some demonstration of the impotence of the Northern Democrats and influenced
the return of Negro votes to the Republicans in the 1956 elections. The Negro's cause is such that what is done about the
South is as great a concern of the Northern Negro voter no
matter what may be the rewards for party support in the North.
The Kennedy administration has shown no disposition to sympathize with the oligarchy, regardless of its power for evil. What
this administration may find to be necessary compromises has
not yet appeared.

Organized labour, particularly the industrial unions, has given
comfort and support to desegregation. An ominous threat to
organized labour is that proposing extension of 'right-to-work'
legislation. The psychological importance of threatened legislation contrary to the interests of organized labour is not to be dis-
counted. Working people in the South have memories that encourage the acceptance of right-to-work laws as being in their interest. Working-class white men remember that at one time skilled
work in the South was a monopoly of slave artisans. Their
fathers have told them of the fight made to get the craft unions
organized to give white workers opportunity to follow their
trades. The 'white only' membership clauses in the by-laws of
these unions were designed to protect this opportunity for them-

selves and their children. Of very recent memory are the court suits and the warning murders of Negro railway workers in the effort to preempt railroad operating jobs for white workers. The craft unions have an obligation to the oligarchy for the legal arrangements that supported them. Among these white workers there is the annoyance of a lingering belief that there are employers in the South who would prefer Negro workers to themselves. Negro workers too have memories that incline them to sympathy for right-to-work laws. Their memories are those of their sufferings at the hands of the lily-white unions.

At this time of a labour market glutted with workers eliminated from agriculture, with distrust of unions on the part of Negroes and a distrust of inter-racial unions on the part of whites, organized labour is deeply concerned about the new industries in the South. Threats of laws and law enforcement officials arrayed against them understandably give organized labour pause in making an alliance with Negroes.

Church allies of the Negro are not exempt from the attention of the oligarchy. Most of the threats to religious groups are a muttered or whispered smear. To claim that the Christian ministry is subversive, and then to give the charge a denial that only advertises it, is cunning. Before the communist label became such a popular all-purpose derogation, the oligarchy had smears such as that described in the following story:

At one time in Nashville, Tennessee, Dr Charles S. Johnson conducted a seminar for Fisk University students on the *Negro In America* at the same school term that Dr Alva W. Taylor conducted a seminar at the Vanderbilt School of Religion on *Race Relations*. Once a month the two student groups met together.

A student minister who pastored a church in a small town nearby invited several of the Fisk students to visit his church services. One Sunday evening a half-dozen of them attended the services of this church.

At the next monthly joint session of the seminars, the young minister reported on his having been dismissed by his congregation. He said that he first became aware of sentiment against him when a leading layman was trying to get across the meaning of the concept 'Anti-Christ'. Finally he said, 'I can easy tell you what an Anti-Christ is: An Anti-Christ is a preacher that will bring a nigger into your church.'

Some denominations, including the Catholics, Episcopalians, and Presbyterians, have been aggressive in creating sentiment among their memberships and among the American people against segregation. Methodist women's organizations and Mrs M. E. Tilly's *Fellowship of the Concerned* carried on quietly effective work for betterment of race relations. Attacks on these groups by the oligarchy and the threat of attention to be given them by the Un-American Activities Committee of the Congress challenge Christian fortitude.

Negroes have a new weapon with respected fire-power. This is appeal to world opinion. Until World War II it made little impact. Suddenly it became of tremendous importance. The movements of liberation among colonial peoples in Asia and Africa together with a United States foreign policy that had this nation assume a role of leadership of the democratic forces in the world made the Negro's grievances at home significant. The United States as a knight with a sword of justice at the service of all in trouble could not explain away a shackled Negro in its own courtyard. Negroes have exploited this threat to national prestige and world influence as ruthlessly as the oligarchy has exploited its domestic advantage. Negroes have wandered to far places in the world, defending the 'American Way' and in doing so have put claim on Americans to observe more precisely the letter and spirit of the Way at home. In the world struggle Americans are sensitive to news in the papers of Karachi, Peiping, New Delhi, Moscow, and Nairobi. Circulation of unfavourable news can be prevented by preventing the occurrence of unfortunate events. The oligarchy's suggestion that censorship curtains the events appears to be impractical. Neither the oligarchy nor most other Americans can comfortably reply to the Negro's question, 'Why should we fight to give people on the other side of the world what we don't have at home?' There are those who suggest to Negroes that they should tell these people afar how many automobiles Negroes have in the United States, rather than reveal their lack of dignity and peace of spirit.

Suggested, but not yet described, is the battle-ground upon
which this conflict rages. The scenes of battle and deployment
of forces are the media of communication, chiefly the newspapers and magazines. Both the combatants have their media
through which they build the morale of their forces. The Negro
weekly newspapers keep up the morale and keep the Negro
forces informed of the progress of the conflict on its far-flung
battle fronts. Southern weekly and daily papers are considered
as serving the same purpose for the oligarchy. Since both Negroes and whites read the metropolitan dailies in the South these
may serve to bolster the morale of the oligarchy while under-
mining that of the Negroes. The oligarchy tries to limit the
distribution of news and ideas unfavourable to it in its domain.
Distributors of Negro weeklies may be discouraged from selling
them. When a white daily paper shows itself to be unsympath-
etic to the oligarchy's cause efforts may be made to discourage
it. *Time* magazine for April 2, 1956, reports the experiences of
the editor of a southern daily who was 'moderate', to the distaste
of the oligarchy. Intimidation and violence used against the
staff of the paper found approval in a formal denouncement by
the County Democratic convention which called the paper 'The
carpetbagger press'. Discouraged, the editor wrote:

'Editorials that do not speak sedition, bigotry, white supremacy and incitation to legislative folly and physical violence
are not accepted as "honest" or "courageous".'

The oligarchy insists that in its area the views to be given and
the slanting of news reports is to be in its interest.

The struggle for the minds and sentiments of Americans
becomes most meaningful as it appears in magazines with
national circulation and in large metropolitan dailies outside of
the South. The oligarchy and the Negro are pleased when its
side of a question is given currency through the columns of
these periodicals. Both are resentful when angling of the reports
presents its image and its actions in an unfavourable light.

The Negro seldom finds himself at a disadvantage in straight
news accounts of what is happening in the South. The bare
facts seem to create a favourable impression of the Negro. The

peculiarities of Southern law, quaint behaviour in Southern courts, and irresponsible lawless acts by the oligarchy are regarded as making the Negro appear good by contrast. The oligarchy does have the advantage of occupying public office and, from that vantage point, names make news.

On the other hand, Negroes consider themselves to be presented in an unfavourable light in interpretative articles that appear in both magazines and newspapers. Since 1954 the only major article written by a Negro to appear was by Charles S. Johnson in *The New York Times Magazine*. Numerous articles have appeared in magazines, written by whites of many different opinions. The authors of many of these, including Hodding Carter, James F. Byrnes, and T. R. Waring, are forthright in their hostility to the Negro's aspirations. Some of the white writers identify themselves, or are identified by the editors, as 'moderates'. Negroes are frequently unhappy in having their case presented by 'moderates' or 'liberals' whom they surely would not identify as being either moderate or liberal. More Southern daily papers are taking an editorial position against the oligarchy. Ralph McGill writing in the *Atlanta Constitution* batters away at the dishonesty of Southern politicians and foolish positions taken by them.

The editors of *Harper's Magazine* gave space for the presentation of *The Southern Case Against Desegregation*. The author, T. R. Waring, honestly states his purpose to be that of disabusing the minds of prejudiced Northerners for the good of the cause he represents. Since he scatters through his paragraphs all the stereotypes dear to the oligarchy, his claim to be a moderate appears a little dubious. A local group of the oligarchy, the Florence County Convention, soon betrayed Mr Waring in the adoption of a resolution praising him and his paper, *The Charleston News and Courier*, for the paper's stand against forces seeking to bring about racial integration. A similar commendation of the newspaper came from the White Citizens Council of a South Carolina small town. The editors of *Harper's* at the time the article appeared had taken pains to point out the author's errors of fact and logic. Most editors do not undertake to make comment on the half-truths and innuendo with which these articles are often crowded. Negroes are sometimes surprised by friends unknown

to them who are presented as liberals or moderates who proceed
to shoot off their right arm in great kindliness to prevent the
oligarchy from killing them.

The metropolitan dailies in their coverage reflect editorial
policy. Negroes feel that the Negro's side of the controversy will
get a full hearing in the columns of the *New York Post*, the
Washington Post-Time Herald, the *Chicago Sun-Times*, and
the *Los Angeles Mirror-News*. They feel that the *Washington
Star*, the *Chicago Tribune*, the *Los Angeles Times,* and the
Hearst papers are committed to ensure that the oligarchy shall
be heard beyond the borders of the South. The *New York Times*
is in a category by itself because Negroes feel that the very
policy of giving full coverage of events favours them. Reporters
for these and other Northern and Western dailies are not *per se*
good or bad for anybody's cause. When Negroes have the opportunity to take them to its favoured vantage points and show
them what is to be seen they applaud their services. When the
members of the oligarchy are able to determine the vantage
point from which they view the scene they applaud their
services.

In their accounts, the reporters reveal as much about themselves as they do about the subject that they report. One
reporter will be grateful for the assistance of a Southern policeman in showing him the Negro section of a city. His story of
his visit to the Negro ghetto will carry the flavour of the policeman's commentary and what is reported will reveal that the
reporter's eyes focused where the policeman pointed. A reporter
who writes paragraphs like the following raises some question
about his sophistication.

'And why is it (to look at the other side of the coin for a
moment) that the Negro, if he wants to live with the white,
turns down the chance when it is offered? '

'For years, they say, the rich white families of Birmingham
have offered good upstairs rooms to their maids and butlers,
good furniture and a radio, the saving of thirty-four cents a
day bus fare and many dollars in rent—and yet not one maid
or butler in fifty will live with the white families, each one
announcing in a whisper, with eyes downcast, that if Madame

doesn't mind we would prefer to go on living in the shacks of Tuxedo Junction.'

'Why? The Southern Negro living in a white house feels that he is in a plush strait-jacket.'

The whole issue of segregated housing is lost in this account, and the idea of a strait-jacket has nothing at all to do with a person living where he wants to, as he wants to without someone else limiting him to a narrow choice. So much is slurred over in such an account as to obscure the issue which is: can a Negro middle-class person move into the house next door and discuss with *his* servants whether they want to live in or not? Such reporting clouds the atmosphere in which the public affair is considered.

Both the Negro and the oligarchy are disturbed when reporters' accounts seem to them to create an atmosphere hostile to the advancement of their cause. The reporter who finds the governor of the state or the chief of police of the city to be really a nice guy who simply can't escape from imperatives of the situation which he must respect reluctantly but firmly, will write with a sympathy for the official that makes Negroes unhappy over the sympathy the account is earning abroad for the enemy. The reporter who spends time with Negro leaders and finds them intelligent, pleasant people distresses the oligarchy as much. The reporter who goes to one interview announcing that he did so hoping to peek into a Negro's heart appears to have some odd notion about open-door hearts. One reporter goes to the Negroes who have petitioned for admission of their children to a white school and in his report disperses, to their satisfaction, the impression they would give. Another reporter goes to Negroes selected by the local school officials and disperses impressions that the school officials would give. It is revealing when a reporter goes to a Negro school administrator, who is careful to get permission of his superiors to talk to the reporter, and then proceeds to tell him that Negroes are not really concerned about school desegregation—to have the reporter then disperse this impression as the Negro's views on the subject.

The space being given to news of what is happening in the South and what Southerners are doing on the national scene is evidence that a great many people in America are interested in the subject. To repeat again President Wilson's observation, that newsmen are a crucial factor in creation of the atmosphere for this public affair and are responsible for the dispersal of the right impression, is to emphasize the concern of both sides of the controversy for what the reporters write. When Southern newsmen welcome them with the handclasp of a brother in the trade, Negroes look at them askance. These Southern newsmen have expressed appreciation for the visitors as being understanding and performing a service by giving the rest of the nation a better view of the South's problems. When they speak in this fashion, Negroes are troubled because they distrust any reporter whose accounts are approved by the papers of the South that are vehicles for the views of the oligarchy. The oligarchy has won a victory when these 'moderate' or 'open-minded' newsmen report a situation or an incident prefaced by the oligarchy's perspective of it, and followed by the oligarchy's interpretation of it.

What prize is to be won by all this news and commentary directed to Americans outside of the South? Negroes are convinced that beliefs and behaviour patterns fostered by the oligarchy are being spread all over the country. They fear the result of comfort given latent prejudices indigenous to the North and West by any triumph of the oligarchy. While they, Negroes, are winning legal support for their cause in the South, the oligarchy is winning the sentiments of more and more people outside of the South. The oligarchy expresses almost the opposite view. It has been left to its devices because people in the rest of the country sympathized with it and felt it should be so left. It feels the inroads on the sentiments of people outside of the South by Negroes are no less a threat to it than the Negro's legal victories.

The oligarchy is making a massive effort in launching its counter-offensive. The senior Senator from Virginia who holds office by votes of less than one-third of the potential voters in his state admonished his adherents, 'If we show the proper fortitude' the justices of the Supreme Court may 'have good cause to reverse themselves and may recognize that they have started something they can't finish.' (*New York Times*, March 19, 1957). The Georgia legislature, in its 1957 session, enacted legislation for a 'sell-the-Georgia-story advertising campaign'. Representative John Bell Williams of Mississippi, speaking on February 8, 1957, to the Sumter, S. C. County White Citizens Councils said : 'Peace and understanding, enlightenment and fundamental American-ism will have to be our battle cry as we seek to enlist friends and allies throughout the rest of the nation.' (*Southern School News*, March, 1957).

Contumacious in their dissidence, the oligarchy has remained in cold rebellion against the government of the United States since the stilled guns at Appomattox ended military rebellion. When, at long last, an American generation becomes committed to the extension of the national law and authority over the rebel-lious, the rebels are determined to resort to the refined arts of psychological warfare. Representatives of the oligarchy have been forthright in their declaration to convince the rest of the nation of the rightness of their sustained revolt. Legislatures, governors, and publicists in the ranks of the oligarchy are about this task of putting good countenance on what is simply rebellion.

CHAPTER VIII

The Price of Disrespect for Law

The successful legal system is one whose principles are generally accepted and whose specific regulations are such that the law-breaker suffers guilt of conscience. His fear of punishment is grounded in anticipated justice. When social change necessitates prescribing or proscribing behaviour in the new situation these are accepted, prior to their proved need, because of faith obtaining in the system of legal safeguards of the community and the person.

The unsuccessful legal system is one about whose principles there is controversy; about whose specific regulations there is resentment; where the fear of punishment is related to suspicion of capricious injustice; where the offender defends his offence in good conscience; and the new proscription is regarded as annoyance or tyranny. The lawmakers discount the intelligence and distrust the morality of those for whose guidance they legislate, excluding themselves. When those for whom laws are made discount the good faith of the makers and come to lose sight of the boundary between just and unjust laws they become corrupted with resentment against all law and the social order that law imposes.

' A man who makes laws for other people which he himself has no disposition to respect must act like a devil for he feels himself to be a God.'

SETTING aside any unjust blame given the oligarchy for many things, and any unmerited praise it may receive, credit for laws made and their enforcement may not be denied those who govern. Whether the laws are written with wisdom and enforced with feeling mercy or to the harsh letter, the respect given the laws by those who use them as the instrument for governing and

98

by those they govern determines the peace of the community and the tranquillity of the citizen. In any account given of its stewardship over the South, the oligarchy must include the framework of laws within which the people of the South exist.

No sphere of activity of the oligarchy is less subject to misinformation or misunderstanding than that of law-making and law enforcement. The record is clear, specific, and available in an open file of statute books and court records. Charges that the oligarchy has produced a troublesome legal system by the enactment of 'laws' without responsibility can conveniently be validated or disproved. Five charges may be given attention: 1. The oligarchy has made laws designed to proscribe some of the relations between classes of citizens but not other relations between the same classes. 2. It has made laws proscribing relations across class lines that are not proscribed within class lines. 3. It has made laws applicable to local communities only, which are at variance with laws in other local communities. 4. It has made laws that are inequitable in their specifying application to some classes of people while exempting others. 5. It has made laws that are unique in their variance with or contradiction to federal law. The result has been confusion of the law-abiding and contempt of the law-making.

Laws enacted by the oligarchy have been placed on the statute books with a speed and ease that democratic government might envy. Since these laws require neither validation by referenda, whereby those to whom they apply may express approval, nor the opportunity to disapprove or endorse law-makers by vote of the people, enactment may be swift and application prompt. When the United States Supreme Court ruled in 1945 that Democratic Party primary elections could not be limited to white voters, the legislature of South Carolina promptly passed an act abolishing the primary. Since the school integration decision of the Supreme Court in 1954, several state legislatures in the South have legisled their public school systems out of existence, should implementation of the decision be undertaken. For a decade now, at each session, some state legislatures have passed peculiar laws having to do with voter qualifications or prescribing conditions of voter registration—all aimed to deter Negroes from voting. These 'laws' will hardly stand up when their validity is given a court test but they are on the statute books. In order to become a registered voter in Alabama the prospective voter must secure the sponsorship of an already registered voter. In Mississippi he must read and interpret the Constitution. Each session of the state legislatures since the 1954 school decision has produced some rather bizarre 'laws'.

The Alabama legislature, among its other acts, has declared the the school desegregation rulings of the U.S. Supreme Court 'null, void, and of no effect'. Among the score of laws passed by the Georgia legislature is one that takes away the retirement and disability benefits of state officials who do not enforce segregation laws. In the litter of legislation by the Mississippi legislature is a law abolishing compulsory school attendance. The South Carolina legislature has given the County Sheriff authority to remove and assign pupils to schools. The Virginia legislature passed a law that no federal employee, except minor employees and clerks, can serve on school boards.

Segregation laws are too many and too diverse to describe or even to list. However, those that vary from city to city confuse those who would obey them. In some situations the Negro servants of white people are exempted from segregation laws. In some cities Negroes and whites may attend a public meeting together provided an aisle separates them; in others they may not sit on the same floor or level of the building. In some cities Negroes and whites may participate together in athletic contests, while in others they may not.

The great problem which the 'laws' of the South present does not arise from the celebrated crimes against person or property, or even those involving constitutional rights, but from the 'legally' defined misdemeanors and lesser felonies charged against Negroes so as to plague them in their day-by-day living. Such laws and their enforcement can make life unduly complex and most inconvenient. Uncounted vexations arise from 'laws' applying to:

> *Where a Negro may dwell*
> *Where he may eat.*
> *Where he may ride on a public conveyance.*
> *What door to a public place he may enter.*

A travel case that attracted attention a few years ago involved Dr Charlotte Hawkins Brown, President of the Palmer Memorial Institute in North Carolina. Dr Brown had gone with a group of professional colleagues, who were white, to a meeting in Mexico. On the return trip Dr Brown was refused passage across Texas with her party because the separate railway coach law of Texas forbade it. She appealed to her fellow North Carolinian, the Honourable Josephus Daniels, then Ambassador to Mexico. Mr Daniels sought to intercede with the railroad officials. The officials found an exception that might be used: if Dr Brown would don a maid's cap and apron she could continue her journey in the company of her party. Negro nursemaids and attendants to white passengers were permitted to travel with them. The lady college president did not choose to be a nursemaid for a day in Texas.

Towards the end of World War II, Negro military policemen were taking German prisoners of war from one military installation to another for incarceration. At Atlanta, Georgia they had a stop for meals. It was against the law for the restaurant in the railroad station to serve Negroes. The German prisoners were welcome to eat. The military policemen were told they could guard their prisoners by covering the exits from the restaurant.

Several years ago the United States Supreme Court banned segregation in inter-state travel, but all public carriers have not accepted this ban. Jim Crow accommodations are still provided and some bus drivers and train conductors make it unpleasant for Negroes who refuse to accept seats in the segregated space. City ordinances and state laws remain in effect requiring segregation according to race in travel within states and cities. In some cities bus drivers are deputized and charged with enforcement of segregation laws. In others the police officer is readily available to arrest a passenger, on complaint of the bus driver, for refusing to abide by the law.

Disturbing the peace of the southern community is remarkably easy. It appears to be an uneasy peace indeed. In one southern city a Negro host was arrested and fined for having white dinner guests in his home. His dinner party constituted a threat to the peace of the community. A Negro who gets into

an argument with a white salesman in a store may be fined
for breach of the peace. Outside a Negro cafe in Carrollton,
Georgia there was for years a four by six foot sign that read:
'NO LAUGHING OR LOUD TALKING', by order of the Mayor
and City Commissioners.'

Into such 'laws' as these on the state statute books and among
city ordinances there is written a disrespect for the basic law
of the nation.

Americans outside of the South take little account of these
small matters. More familiar to them are the notorious 'miscarriages of justice' in which the laws of the states that are in
consonance with federal law are inequitably applied. The sensational cases that have had front-page coverage in the daily
papers include the 'Scottsboro Case' in the 1930's, the 'Wright
Case' in the 1940's and the 'Till Case' in the 1950's. In these
cases the question was not of law as it is written but of the interpretation and application of the law. Newspaper coverage in
these instances placed Southern courts and Southern governors
on trial before public opinion while the cases ran their legal
course. Should capital crimes such as murder or rape be proved,
severe punishment to fit the crime would be expected. However,
the use of the power of the courts and that of the state executive
in the application of the law left many people aghast over the
manner in which law could be manipulated.

Enforcement of law rests ultimately with the courts. There
errors in charges made, or abuse of the police power may be
remedied. Flagrant abuse of the judicial power and trial by jury
were revealed in these celebrated cases in recent history. Until
the Emmet Till Case, the most notorious travesty on justice was
the trial of the 'Scottsboro Boys' on a charge of rape. These
nine Negro youths were arrested on a charge of having raped
two white women, who happened to have been their fellow
hoboes on a freight train. They were promptly brought to trial,
convicted, and on April 9, 1931 eight of them were sentenced
to die by electrocution on June 10th of that year. The Supreme
Court of Alabama confirmed the sentences. The Supreme Court
of the United States reviewed the cases and ordered new trials.
In the second trial in 1933, they were again convicted and the
judge passed sentence as required by the verdict. However, in

granting a petition for a new trial this judge issued one of the most scathing indictments of the abuse of justice in his court to be found in the records.

The Till case has been too much in the news recently to require review. Suffice it to say that in the trial for his murder the defendants admitted to having abducted him while denying having murdered him. After acquittal on the charge of murder the defendants were tried for abduction and acquitted.

The remarkable thing about the Till Case was the publicity that it received. The trial of a white killer of a Negro is rare in the South, to say nothing of his receiving punishment for an act that is seldom defined as being a crime. Unless the deed is done in full view of witnesses, law enforcement authorities have trouble discovering suspects. When the identity of the murderer is known, the grand jury frequently fails to find the act to be one justifying indictment. The occasional white murderer of a Negro who is brought to trial stands small chance of being convicted. The reverse is true of the Negro who kills a white person. Many suspects are found. The grand jury readily finds a true bill. Rarely does the trial jury see any mitigating circumstances and the death penalty is given and carried out.

In a study of homicides in North Carolina, by Professor Guy B. Johnson, it was found that, when Negroes are convicted of killing whites, 42.9 per cent received the death penalty and 11.4 per cent were given life imprisonment. When whites were convicted of killing Negroes, none were sentenced to either death or life imprisonment. When whites were convicted of killing whites 18.6 per cent were sentenced to death and 5.1 per cent to life imprisonment. When Negroes murdered Negroes 6.7 per cent were given the death penalty and 4 per cent were sentenced to life imprisonment.

Leniency towards Negroes for crimes against Negroes was charged against Atlanta, Georgia courts in a letter to the editor of the *Sunday Atlanta Journal and Constitution,* December 10, 1950. The letter was signed by Bishop J. H. Kendrick, Honorary Chairman and Bishop J. H. Calhoun, Chairman, of the Atlanta Commission on Crime Prevention. The chief of detectives in a Texas city complained about the leniency in his city. He said that he believed that if Negroes were on juries Negro offenders would get harsher sentences rather than being turned loose as they were by white juries. His concern was about the pressure put on his staff, who had to apprehend culprits time and again when juries failed to mete out punishment to repeaters.

Crimes of Negroes against Negroes make for the high crime rates in the South. Sporadic studies and general observations have suggested several factors as contributing to this high incidence of crime. One is that the general frustration felt by Negroes in the bi-racial social system is expressed in aggression against other Negroes. A second factor appears to be a pattern of Negroes resorting to violent settlement of differences without recourse to law and the courts that they mistrust. A third factor is the general leniency of the courts and juries when both parties in a crime are Negroes.

In part the Negro crime rate is class behaviour, the behaviour of the economic and socially disadvantaged, but it is complicated by colour. Everywhere it is serious enough when groups acquire their own weapons to settle their own differences according to a code in which the police officer has no place. According to such a code, an aggrieved party who appeals to the police loses face among his fellows. It becomes doubly unfortunate when those disposed to accept this code do so on the basis of colour. This disrespect for law and its enforcement has a high price paid in lives, in property damage, in hospital costs, in time lost from work, in fines the offender is rarely able to pay, and in the costs of maintenance of penal institutions. From the *Uniform Crime Reports for the United States and Its Possessions* for 1950 the arrests of Negroes were greatly out of proportion with their percentage of the population. Of all arrests for carrying weapons, Negroes were 50.1 per cent, for criminal homicide 45.6 per cent, for assault 46.4 per cent. These were arrests and not convictions. Studies of crime in the South reveal that there is the general practice of careless and indiscriminate arresting of Negroes on suspicion of crime. The crime rate is undoubtedly high but the arrest rate is higher. Careless charges and careless punishment contribute to the heavy cost of crime in the

South. Together, those who disrespect the law by failure to give it obedience and those who enforce it carelessly cost America dearly.

In the South there is not only disrespect for law and for the 'laws' but also for 'The Law'. In the small towns and villages The Law is not a set of statutes, but a man in a big hat with a holstered gun slapping his thigh. His word is law and in his person is vested justice, if that may be found in the punishment he dispenses. Whether he is sheriff, sheriff's deputy or constable what he says is the law within his domain and there are none to question his word. When he arrives at a conclusion it is a verdict not to be gainsaid. The Negro suspect's alibi or claim of innocence ends when The Law orders, 'Nigger, don't you dispute my word.' His alleged offence dwindles to unimportance alongside the crime of doubting the perception or challenging the conclusion of this man who regards himself as being The Law.

Sometimes the punishment is made to fit the crime, whether it is to be found in the fine print of the legal code or not. A few years ago when Negro teenagers made efforts to be well-dressed in keeping with the zoot-suit fad, a constable in Texas enjoyed deterring juvenile delinquency. Performance of his official duties did appear to be done in the spirit of sport. He would visit juke-joints in the Negro neighbourhood and have the boys line up and come past him. He sat by the door and with patient good humour slit each trouser leg with a sharp knife as the boys filed out of the place.

In the Southern city the policeman is not considered to be a protector, but a menace. A Negro who had been reared in the Midwest and later came South to live commented on this:

'It gives you the strangest feeling to know that the policeman on the corner is not there to protect you. In Minneapolis I had known a policeman who lived in the next block. He was my friend when I was a kid. I was taught that the policeman is there to protect me from toughs and crooks. Then I come here and find that the policeman is not a friend, that he will abuse me and not protect me, that I must fear him more than toughs or crooks.'

D*

A person can know no tranquillity of spirit so long as it is understood that he is automatically wrong in any altercation with a white person. Neither is tranquillity promoted by the knowledge that the police officer is little concerned about an altercation between two Negroes. Their troubles are an annoyance and the victim may find himself charged with some offence and penalized as quickly as the person against whom he makes a complaint.

Occasionally a police officer is obviously guilty of some act so brutal that resentment is stirred up among white people in the community and he is relieved of his job, but rarely does his punishment go beyond that. Unarmed Negroes in the custody of peace officers too often are killed while 'resisting arrest', 'attacking the arresting officer', or 'trying to escape'. When a peace officer is punished, it is news. In 1950, two Lafayette, Alabama, policemen were sentenced to six months and ten months in federal prison for violating the civil rights of a young Negro they had killed but for whose death a jury had refused to convict them. A Louisiana deputy sheriff was indicted for depriving a prisoner of life without due process of law. Georgia police officers were convicted of handing prisoners over to a Ku Klux Klan group for flogging.

In those big court cases involving civil rights, when the attention of the nation is focused on the proceedings, the judicial proprieties are meticulously observed. In the thousands of little cases the court atmosphere is different. A Negro charged with an offence is frequently advised by his attorney to plead guilty and seek the mercy of the court. The arresting officers determined to make a good case may so relate the circumstances as to make the charge appear to be a substantial one. To challenge the officer's version is to alienate the magistrate and to lay the litigant open to future harassment by the officer challenged. No man could be so unfortunately marked as the Negro characterized by police officers as 'smart' or 'uppity'. It may be observed that in the civil rights cases and in the cases of sensational miscarriages of justice a Southern white lawyer is seldom among the attorneys for the Negro. In the run-of-the-mill cases the Negro's attorney does himself no good in being too diligent in his client's behalf. The local lawyer who is foolhardy enough to impugn the testimony of a white witness, reminds the judge of points of law that could well be ignored, or otherwise makes too a good case for his client, may expect reprisals from his neighbours.

Some unbelieving reader may be revolted by the accounts of them and choose to question the author's sensibilities and fairness in giving such a report. Awareness of their occurrence is necessary and they take on significance when viewed in relation to the Negro's status under the written law and before 'The Law' incarnate.

In a consideration of the operation of the law and the 'laws' the importance of the ballot may not be dismissed. At various periods it has been argued by conservatives that education, or economic security, should be given priority over the ballot and political participation on the Negro's agenda for the advancement of his cause. The argument has been, 'Leave politics alone; get ready and the vote will come.' The fact remains that government is responsive to those with the power to sustain or remove it.

Fifteen years have passed since the Supreme Court of the United States lifted the ban on Negroes from voting in the Democratic Party primaries. Various devices have been employed subsequently in an effort to keep the electorate restricted. When all legal devices and legal subterfuges have been exhausted, intimidation and the 'slow-down' remain as effective means of withholding the ballot. In Alabama boards of registrars have simply moved with deliberate speed in certifying the eligibility of Negro voters and in placing their names on the voter lists. In 1952 some 6,000 Negroes sought to register in the city of Montgomery. Less than five hundred of this number succeeded in getting themselves enrolled. Such a practice seems incredible to people in a state like California, where the greatest possible registration is sought and registrars sit on street corners or place themselves conveniently in super-markets.

An obligation of the citizen which many citizens seek to avoid as being an inconvenient chore, is jury service. That some people should sue for the opportunity to perform this duty seems strange to many people outside of the South. Yet Southern Negroes have sought jury service as a citizenship right. It was on appeal to the Supreme Court of the United States by one of the defendants in the Scottsboro case that systematic exclusion of Negroes from jury service was taken into account. The court forbade the exclusion of Negroes from jury lists. While Negroes may not be denied jury duty by federal law, the appearance of a Negro on a jury in the South is still sufficiently rare for it to be news. Respect for law is sadly impaired, when The Law may accuse, to suit its whim, of violation of 'laws', and when defence lawyers must take care not to defend before jurymen whose common philosophy of life precludes impartial deliberation on the case.

The second-class citizen who does not have the use of the ballot also finds his access to public services limited. The simplest conveniences that are taken for granted. elsewhere become a serious issue for Negroes in the South. Street lights, sewage disposal, street paving, and access to the municipal water supply, demanded elsewhere, must be begged for by Southern Negroes. Mute but eloquent testimony as to differential provision of public services may be given by a farm-to-market road in the rural South. The hard surface on such a road ends at the last dwelling of a white farmer, that is, just before the homes of the Negro farmers begin. Without the ballot these Negroes can only plead for such services.

When the Negro cannot demand his rights, he may secure some benefits as privileges through the good offices of a kindly disposed white person who will interest himself in the Negro's behalf. The very security and well-being of Negroes in many communities depend upon the intercession of their white friends. There are limits within which this intercession must be confined if the friendly advocate is to escape the displeasure of the oligarchy. White men of goodwill, or at least those who would secure for Negroes more protection from the law, are not themselves exempt from feeling pressure from those who rule. Those who would encourage Negroes to seek enjoyment of the rights and privileges do so with tortured misgivings. The public position of Nobel prize-winner William Faulkner is a case in point.

In his *Letter to the North* through the pages of *Life* magazine, Mr Faulkner had to say,

'. . . the South will go to any length, even the fatal and already doomed one, before it will accept alteration of its racial condition by mere force of law or economic threat.'

Prior to this in the *Letter*, he had admitted,

'There are more Southerners than I who believe as I do and have taken the same stand I have taken, at the same price of contumely and insult and threat from other Southerners which we foresaw and were willing to accept because we believed we were helping our native land which we love, to accept a new condition which it must accept whether it wants to or not.'

Months before, Mr Faulkner had written a letter that appeared in Southern papers encouraging compliance with the desegregation decision of the United States Supreme Court. In replying to comments on his *Letter to the North*, Mr Faulkner defended it by saying,

'The reason behind the letter was the attempt of an individual to save the South and whole United States too from the blot of Miss Autherine Lucy's death. She had just been suspended by the University of Alabama; a day had been set when a judge would pass on the validity of the suspension, which he would have to do, the forces supporting her attempt to enter the university would send her back to it. I believe that if they did so, she would possibly lose her life.'

Mr Faulkner, in this exchange, indicates that the first Negro student admitted to the University of Alabama stood a chance of losing her life for the attempt. Protection for her could not be expected and no man of good will would like to consider that a word of encouragement from him should be a note in a siren song luring her to death.

A prominent Southern newspaper editor pleaded with Negroes not to sue to enter the university in his state. He was frank in saying that he feared the reprisals the Negro community would be subjected to when a Negro sought this admission. Southern whites who defend federal law against state 'laws' or make intercession in the Negro's behalf do so at the sacrifice of some rights and privileges to which their whiteness entitles them. The thanks they get are few. When the identification 'nigger lover' becomes attached to one of them, to all intents and purposes his effectiveness as a white man is gone. The shield of southern 'laws' no longer covers such a man. The role of the pariah is not a happy one. The story of these men who suffer indignity for the Negro's cause remains to be told. One thing that makes their position uncomfortable, and sometimes terrifying, is that they are in communication with the members of the oligarchy and know its ruthlessness and the helplessness of those who suffer its displeasure. The distinguished Dr Frank P. Graham, University President, Senator, diplomat, has been shown many discourtesies by his fellow North Carolinians for his unorthodox view on race relations.

For taking a position of moderation, Governor James E. Folsom of Alabama risked reprisal and met its attempt. His avowal that law and order would be preserved at the University of Alabama brought from the Citizens Councils the initiation of a petition to impeach him. Affirmation of his belief in segregation was not enough. He had consistently refused to align himself with the extremists. Without their Governor's blessings the extremists had found it necessary to import Senator Eastland of Mississippi, former Governor Talmadge of Georgia, and his successor, Governor Griffin, to build their morale. These extremists translated the suggestion that police protection at the University of Alabama constituted encouragement of Miss Autherine Lucy to persist in her efforts to become a student there.

Former Governor Bibb Graves of Alabama has been condemned for his 'welshing' on a promise to free the last of the Scottsboro Boys, who languished in prison while Alabama 'laws' vengefully delayed their release. As Dr Allan Knight Chalmers gives the account of this broken promise, Governor Graves becomes a pitiable figure. His fellows in the upper echelons of the oligarchy in Alabama would not permit him to carry out his promise. Mrs Eleanor Roosevelt telephoned him encouragement to carry it out. President Roosevelt, whom the Governor admired greatly, invited him to join the President at Warm

Springs for Thanksgiving holiday. Governor Graves did not accept the invitation and avoided a meeting with the President in which he would be asked about his promise. In a final interview with Dr Chalmers the Governor is reported as saying, 'I can't go through with it. I am finished politically if I do.'

Governor Graves was doubtless correct. Judge James E. Horton did pay the price for his rebuke of the oligarchy for its machinations in the Scottsboro case. He was voted out of office and preached out of the communion of respectable Southerners.

In 1956, Dr Guy H. Wells, President Emeritus of Georgia State College for Women, was accused of being in favour of integration of schools and stripped of his honorific title by the state Board of Regents of Georgia. The regents further asked that the Teacher Retirement Board of the state discontinue Dr Wells' $518.93 monthly pension. Indicating his approval of these reprisals, the Governor of Georgia commented that Dr Wells 'has been acting a little ugly'.

There are men of moderation within the oligarchy and men of goodwill outside of it who have made personal sacrifices for government under law, and in doing so they have allied themselves with the Negro's cause. They will be remembered as forces of conscience in the white community. In critical instances they have been martyrs to the cause, even though their very lives were not required for its furtherance. To name them here in gratitude would be a kiss of persecution.

Negroes know this. Their long patience in the use of appeal and court action shows their awareness. They know that drastic action would cast them in the role of the rebel, which the oligarchy now occupies, and lose sympathy for their efforts. Negroes seek to enjoy the rights and privileges they want. They are not heroes and martyrs obsessed with making a sacrifice of life to the cause. History records few heroes and martyrs to be honoured and revered long past the age in which they made their sacrifice. There are Negroes who have given life, livelihood and security in the struggle for their 'rights'. White men of moderation within the oligarchy and those of goodwill outside of it along with Negroes are fearful because they know that the law-enforcers may not be depended upon to use their power to uphold law and preserve order.

In one large Southern city citizens of high prestige and no small influence undertook the sponsorship and planning of an inter-racial conference of college students. The publisher of the largest daily paper, the president of the local television station, and the executive vice-president of a bank formed a committee to clear the way for the conference with city officials. The newspaper publisher reported the results of their efforts to the full planning committee:

We saw the police commissioner. He gave permission for the conference without having to observe the segregated seating ordinance. The only condition he made was that white and Negro students use separate rest rooms. As long as they do that everything will be all right.

Now the commissioner has taken personal responsibility for policing the affair. He has picked a special squad of policemen to handle anything that may come up in connection with the conference. He has instructed the desk sergeant at police headquarters to give any calls about the meeting to this special squad. No other officers are to be sent out there. As a matter of fact other policemen have been instructed to remain away from the vicinity. The commissioner is not sure how the rank and file of police officers would take this kind of gathering.

In most cities gentlemen with the prestige and influence of these would hold the police commissioner accountable for the orderly conduct of an enterprise that they sponsored. In this city they could not, and the police commissioner himself could not give assurance of the discipline of the police force he directed.

An atmosphere of insecurity and fear is created when those who hold political power give evidence that they do not respect law. This situation obtains so long as those having power consider law as an instrument of power ready to their use in their own interests and in such interest only. When a law does not serve their purpose they refuse to enforce it. If need be they make another law to suit their whim. To cloak their machinations in a guise of legality they remove a law to make one. It is not surprising that the members of the oligarchy denounce the Supreme Court of the United States. In their states and communities they make and use 'laws'; they are not subject to law.

Until the Freedom Riders, mob action had all but disappeared in the South. Its purposes can be achieved more efficiently under a cloak of spurious legality. The pattern of mass performance of extra-legal punishment became embarrassing to the oligarchy, whose apologies for these deeds became monotonous and rang hollow in the ears of the world. Questions were raised about governments, state and local, whose officials lamely excused destruction of life and property as the work of the faceless lower classes. Too long did they deplore and decry the lynching party and the mob while excusing themselves as the 'best' people who do not share in such activity. They could never explain away in acceptable disclaimers their failure to exercise their responsibility for deterring those who did indulge in the activity.

The self-described people, into whose hands have been committed the exercise of government functions, cannot disclaim responsibility for the laws they make or the manner in which they are applied. The oligarchy may not disclaim responsibility for its members who become prototypes of the 'bully boy'. These characters follow closely the familiar model of the underworld character who makes good by laying down his law in a domain he tyrannizes by use of strong-arm methods. For as long as he endures he swaggers about the scene, intimidating and corrupting police officers, sneering at the law-respecting and cowing the law-abiding. He has an 'organization' of informers and hatchet-men and enjoys a period of despoiling his 'subjects' before doom comes at the hands of some ambitious rival, or he is put away for income-tax evasion. The greatest achievement of this type is the despoilment that comes in the success it has in corrupting young men who, on a grand or minor scale, would be imitators. Far more tragic for America is the bully boy in a governorship or in a legislative seat who shows young men the path to power and success by putting himself above the law. The demonstration of insinuating oneself into control of the legal machinery so as to cynically manipulate it is a chilling spectacle. Right-minded Americans will accord to this type only revulsion, rather than the admiration the neurotic gives the gangster. It is hard to calculate the damage done to respect for law by these personalities in American political life who thrive on shouting defiance at the courts and sneering at the expectation of the naïve that they will enforce laws they do not like.

On Monday, April 23, 1956, the Supreme Court of the United States handed down a decision that segregation on public transportation within states was illegal. The public carrier in Montgomery, Alabama, the Montgomery City Lines, Inc., announced a policy of non-segregation on its buses. The oligarchy in Alabama promptly acted to negate the Supreme Court's decision. Jack Owen, President of the Alabama Public Service Commission, issued *his* decision. First, he issued an order to the owners of the Montgomery City Lines, Inc.:

'I HEREBY DEFY THE RULING HANDED DOWN BY THE U.S. SUPREME COURT. ALABAMA STATE LAW REQUIRING SEGREGATION OF THE RACES ON BUSES STILL STANDS. I DEMAND THAT YOU WITHDRAW YOUR ORDER APPROVING INTEGRATION ON YOUR BUSES IN MONTGOMERY.'

'Tacky' Gayle, Mayor of Montgomery, declared the policy of the government of the city to be unchanged and that it would continue segregation.

Clyde Sellers, Police Commissioner of Montgomery, alerted his police force to support the decisions of Jack Owen and Bill Gayle. He declared that he would personally give the orders for the arrest of any bus drivers and passengers who sought to abide by the Supreme Court decision. He was prepared to use the police power at his disposal to see that the decisions of his two associates were enforced. However, he indicated that he was not simply supporting his superiors out of a sense of responsibility for executing policy. He was being true to divine right that had been conferred on him by the Maker who clothed his bones in a pale skin. He recognized his mandate in the statement that, 'That's the way I feel. I'm a Southern white man and I want to continue to be one.' Lest the legal supports of his whiteness should fail him, he had affiliated with the extra-legal White Citizens Councils.

Tom, Dick, and Harry or Jack, Tacky, and Clyde may have a mandate from a limited group under local laws. Can the American people condone the placing of this mandate above that of a unanimous Court whose members hold appointments from three Presidents of the United States and whose judicial responsibilities have been approved by the Senate of the United States? Can the American people approve of the disruption of the orderly processes of government by a corps of armed and disciplined police officers pledged to obedience to the commands of Tom, Dick, and Harry or Jack, Tacky, and Clyde?

The price America pays for peculiar and special 'laws' is a creeping disrespect for law. Ultimately, the orderly society rests on the respect for law rather than upon its enforcement. Enforcement is encouragement to give it that respect. Some comfort may be taken even from the obstructive legislation of those states seeking to circumvent federal law. This action indicates an underlying respect for law. To the contrary, efforts to impugn the Supreme Court so as to strip it of respect go a long way towards encouragement of disrespect for law and point in the direction of the police state.

The police state exists when laws lacking respect require an extensive and tyrannical police power for their enforcement. The oligarchy insists that to compel southerners to abide by the Supreme Court's decisions would be tyranny if it were not an impossible task. Should Southerners demonstrate that enforcement of law among them is an impossibility, they would have set an example of effective defiance that could well be followed on other issues by people in other areas of the nation. Such a state of compounded dissidence, in which determined groups of people made their own laws and enforced them at their pleasure, would surely invite tyranny as the only means of having uniform impartial law.

There are those who recognize the legality of the Negro's position but appeal to him to go slow in pressing for the application of law, with the argument that he should be willing for the South to be educated to accept courses of action, when these are forbidden by the 'laws' of Southern states and cities. Does either sympathy for those prejudices expressed in these 'laws', or comfort for those who defy application of the law further education in respect for law?

CHAPTER IX

The Price of Knowledge and Skills Withheld

Control of formal education is usually vested in the Church or in the State and sometimes is shared by both. Those admitted to such instruction are prepared for the exercise of power and the discharge of responsibilities essential to the well-being of the society as it is constructed. Those who do not enjoy the advantages of formal instruction are left to acquire simpler knowledge and cruder skills passed from father to son. This knowledge and these skills are those that ensure the carrying on of common pursuits while preserving the condition of a folk dependent on an elite of the learned and specially skilled.

As important as what is taught in a society is what is withheld. To know who withholds what knowledge from whom is to gain insight into the social structure and the ordered ways of a people. Those who would dominate reserve for themselves knowledge of the mysteries and the art of manipulation of the finer skills. The use of this knowledge and the exercise of this art comes to be equated with superiority of breed and endowment with capacity. Access to restricted knowledge is the avenue to power.

THE average person outside of the South might well be expected to pause in the midst of the hullabaloo over desegregation of schools in the South to ask: 'Just what is the fuss all about?' Perfectly reasonable queries to come after this one are: 'Why do Negroes want their children to go to school with white children?' or 'Why are white parents so determined to keep their children from going to the same schools with Negro children?' There may be those who are at a loss to understand how this issue became so intense as to raise questions about the integrity of the United States Supreme Court and seriously

to affect the chances of a candidate for the Presidency of the
United States to become his party's nominee.

Americans everywhere are being made aware of school problems, especially the problems of too few classrooms and too few
teachers. There is a likelihood that many will dismiss the
clamour about schools in the South as being of the same sort,
and thereby an unnecessary ado about something that does not
affect one area but is a common problem with a confusing twist.
The twist is there, but it is an enormous twist. The South has
peculiar and special problems, some of which may not be extri-
cated from the issue of separate schools for white and Negro
children. To have people outside of the South understand the
issues, it appears to be necessary to describe a school system, some
of whose characteristics are entirely unfamiliar to them.

The state governments of the South now stand challenged
before the nation for the manner in which they have discharged
those responsibilities that inhere in the power of the state to
provide for the education of its citizens. The South has long
claimed and had the sympathy of the nation because of the
problems it faced in the discharge of these responsibilities.
Recognition of the magnitude of these problems elicited tolerance for whatever awkwardness was shown in handling them.
Neither their most understanding sympathizers, nor their least
generous critics could deny that the South had an excessive
burden in the numbers of children to be educated there. The
ratio of children to adults is greater in the South than elsewhere
in the nation. In 1950, 38.4 per cent of the population in the
South and 30.8 per cent outside the South was under twenty
years of age. In 1959, the per capita income in the South was
$1,565 as compared to $2,540 in the East and $2,565 in the West.
The South gained sympathy by presenting evidence that the
states there spent a greater proportion of their tax dollars for
education than did states in other sections of the country.

Most of the American people accepted the South's definition
of its problems and accepted its assurances that it was trying to
solve them in good faith. Even those who disagreed with the
logic for maintaining a dual school system accepted it as an unpleasant fact. Regardless of the circumstances in which they
were taught, the children of the South needed learning and

there were those who bestirred themselves to aid their getting it. Conflicting sentiments about the efforts made by the states to provide schools did not prevent those concerned about the welfare of the children from supplementing provisions made by the states. As a result, a system of private schools was developed in the South parallel to that maintained by public funds. These private schools were required because the governments of the states of the South, whether by accident or design, left many children without benefit of formal education.

The helping hands that maintained private schools were those of church missionary groups. Except for the schools operated by the Catholics and a few other denominational bodies these were not parochial schools. The emphasis was not upon maintaining schools in which the faith might be propagated, but a real altruism directed toward the spread of knowledge rather than the Gospel. These schools were different from private schools maintained outside of the South. The private schools outside of the South were maintained for economically and socially advantaged children; those within the South were maintained for children who were economically and socially disadvantaged. Within and outside of the South, private schools supplement those provided by the state. Outside of the South it becomes a quality supplement for those who seek instruction which they consider superior to that offered in the public facility. Within the South it becomes a quantity supplement for those who may not have access to a public facility.

Church people all over the United States became interested in the educational problems of the South. Self-denying young people consecrated themselves to the task of teaching in inhospitable far places in the South. The churches raised funds to support these schools. The needs of the children were reported to them as being so great that the mission societies collected and sent boxes and barrels of clothing to clothe children fittingly so that they could attend classes. It is a prevalent misconception that this aid was enjoyed by Negro children alone, when the fact is that those mission schools surviving today are chiefly for white children in the mountains of the Southern Appalachians. For two generations Negro children were the greater proportion of those who had this aid. A move spread through the mission bodies to pressure the states of the South to assume their lawful responsibility and take over these schools for Negro children. The Southern communities in which these schools were maintained had long been loath to have Negro children receive some of the teachings included in the instruction of these Northern teachers. The two unrelated sentiments worked together to have the private schools state supported.

After seventy-five years it was demonstrated that the efforts of the states of the South and the private schools together had not succeeded in providing the children of the region with an education comparable to that received by children in other parts of the nation. Proof of this condition of inadequacy sounded an alarm that has made the education of the young in the South a matter of national concern. Whether or not those to be educated realize the seriousness of their limitations, and whether or not the governments of the states of the South realize the disadvantage to them of these limitations, the nation has become aware of the seriousness of limitations that handicap one-fourth of its people.

Some facts revealed in the mobilization for World War II were startling. In spite of all the self-praise the South had given itself in publicizing the advances made there in education, and the reports of plummeting figures on illiteracy to the contrary too many of the young men of the South who presented themselves for military service had to be rejected for reasons of 'mental deficiency', a category populated chiefly with those lacking effective literacy.

The South was responsible for approximately three-fourths (73 per cent) of the men rejected for mental deficiency between 1940 and 1945. The painstaking study of Professor Eli Ginzburg, *The Uneducated*, provides statistics to draw a picture in which the South may not take pride. Of the 716,000 men rejected for mental deficiency, 525,520 were from the South. Identified according to race, 283,260 were white and 287,260 were Negroes. Stated as rejections per 1,000 men registered, the rates for the country as a whole: white-25; Negro-152. For the states in the Southeast the rates were: White-52; Negro-202. The highest rejection rates for Negroes were in South Carolina with a rate of 277, and Louisiana with a rate of 247.

It is apparent that both Negroes and whites were educationally disadvantaged when the white rate in the South is double that for the nation as a whole and the Negro rate in the South is one-third greater than the national rate. The effect of educational differentials is suggested when Negroes, who were 33 per cent of the South's population in 1940, were 55 per cent of rejections for illiteracy and the rejection rate per 1,000 in the United States was six times that of whites and in the South four times that of whites. In addition to these rejections, the Army actually inducted 384,000 illiterate men: 220,000 white and 164,000 Negro.

Selective Service reports for the year 1954 show that in five southern states: Alabama, Georgia, Mississippi, North Carolina, and South Carolina more than 30 per cent of the Selective Service registrants were disqualified because they failed to pass the mental test. Only one state outside of the South, Nevada, had as many as 15 per cent of the Selective Service registrants disqualified on the mental test, while none of the Southern states had fewer than 15 per cent to be so disqualified. Outside of the South disqualifications on this test, taken at random, were; California 9.6, Colorado 4.8, Pennsylvania 3.7 and Iowa 1.4.

Problems met in local communities, when called upon to fill quotas during World War II, made people within the South look again at their schools. In one town in the deep South, where the filling of quotas drew unevenly on the young white men, their mothers became aroused and decided to do something about it. One of the mothers reported the experience as having been an exasperating one:

'When the draft calls came, more and more of our boys had to go to fill the quotas because the coloured boys didn't know enough. Some of the ladies at our church talked about it and we decided to help the coloured boys by teaching them.

'There were some of the ladies who had been school teachers and they were willing to give their time and the School Superintendent cooperated with us by providing the books. It was all set up. We were going to use one of the Sunday School rooms at the Methodist Church.

'You may not believe it but we couldn't get a handful of the coloured boys to come to the classes. We tried for two or three weeks but just had to give it up.

'They talk about they want education, but this experience proved to me they don't. They won't take advantage of it when you offer it to them. They're happy to be ignorant. I was always sympathetic when coloured people complained about what their schools didn't have, but this taught me a lesson. When people just want to be ignorant you can't help them.'

When asked about this, young Negro men were amused or contemptuous. Their feelings were expressed in such comments as, 'Who wants to get educated to get killed.' 'The white boys got the education; let them go ahead and use it.' 'They coulda educated us 'fore now but they put it off kinda late.' 'You know its something funny about that: all of a sudden white women get busy to teach you something.'

The Army felt a need to salvage some of the borderline man-power and set up schools within its reception centres. Educa-tional specialists devised a non-verbal test of intelligence and those who rated high on this test were inducted and assigned to Special Training Units. For the stu the educators designed a course of study that was intended to give a man the equivalent of a fourth grade education in twelve weeks. The army had printed its own textbook—*Private Pete.* How many men in uniform from the South puzzled through the experiences of *Private Pete* seeking minimum effective literacy?

The concern generated for the improvement of education in the South emphasized what had long been known—the South needed help. The kind of sporadic aid on a voluntary basis pro-vided by the church-supported schools had demonstrated that this was inadequate. Those who would share the South's edu-cational burden usually saw the first relief to be in the reorganiza-tion of the educational system, so as to have a single unified system of schools.

The South resisted this proposal as suggesting invasion of the sovereignty of the state governments. For the provision of edu-cation these states, like those in the rest of the nation, have included among their government powers those necessary for the maintenance of a system of instruction of the young. To accomplish the desired instruction the state governments made provisions for it in the taxing power, the appointive power, the regulative power, and the police power. Under these powers the state governments may determine who is to be taught, even to the extent that compulsory attendance laws prescribe penalties for the failure of children of specified ages to present themselves for instruction. A minimum of uniformity of instruction is provided for in the regulation of the time to be given to instruction : hours daily, days annually, and the number of years this schedule is to be followed. State regulations specify what shall be taught and who shall be permitted to teach. Through its taxing power the state government is empowered to provide the funds necessary for the maintenance of schools in which instruction shall be given. The state governments of the South have shown themselves to be jealous of these prerogatives. They defy any encroachment on them and all others may honestly deny responsibility for the manner in which they have been used.

Along with recognition of education as being a government function the assertion of state responsibility for it was made on the basis of the principle of States' rights. Included among these rights was the right to segregate children according to racial identity in separate schools. When the States' rights principle was accepted as valid, a set of rationalizations for segregation were superimposed on it. The third step was the addition of a rationale for differentials in the separate provisions.

Rationalization of the provision of separate schools in which the contents of instruction are different and the emphasis on aspects of instruction are different take several forms:

1. The assumption was stated that the Negro is mentally inferior and therefore incapable of learning what is taught to white children. Therefore to present to Negro children the same instruction given white children is a hopeless task foolishly undertaken.

2. The Negro child is disabled by experience and circumstance for the level of instruction maintained in the schools

for white children. It would handicap the white child and place an undue strain on the Negro child to place them in classes together. It is as much to the Negro child's advantage as it is to that of the white child to teach them separately so that each may learn at a tempo that is comfortable for each.

3. Inherent ability and circumstantial capability are beside the point. The restricted opportunity in the society for the use of knowledge by the Negro child makes the teaching of some things wasteful. It is sheer nonsense to teach children something that they will never have the opportunity to use. More than that—having such knowledge may actually be detrimental if it produces a person who is dissatisfied with his ascribed status. It is really morally wrong to educate a person beyond his station in life.

4. The separate school produces a better adjusted person who can be of greater service to his own people and by giving him useful knowledge he is better equipped to earn a living and find employment.

These rationalizations make it clearly apparent that segregation of schools providing for separation on the basis of racial identity has become a social device for withholding knowledge from one group while giving that knowledge to the other group. This fact is the key, the very crux, of the situation of segregated schools.

In the course of ninety years it succeeded in erecting a great barrier between the Negro school and the white school in the South. Hidden from the view of people outside of the South was the fact that the segregation of schools was a mechanism for admitting some of the young to knowledge while withholding it from other of the young. The discerning in the South are aware of this. The President of a Negro land-grant college discussing the institution to which he had given many years of service summed up his problems in the simple statement that: 'The Negro land-grant college was designed and operated so as never to teach a Negro anything that would put him a competition with a white man.' Negroes are nonplussed when credulous people take seriously the smoke-screen raised by those who support segregation such as: 'The door to the schoolroom is the door to the bedroom.' or 'I oppose integrated schools because I don't want a little burr-head calling me "Grandpa".' They know, and those who seek to divert attention from the real issue know, that the door to the schoolroom is the door to better jobs, higher pay, and to participation in government. It is to prevent these things that the segregated school system is preserved.

In order to have segregated schools there must be a sanction on the part of the dominant group in the society and a sanction on the part of the subordinate group. It is readily obvious that the governments and the influential white people in the South sanction school segregation and that until recently Negroes have sanctioned it. The dual system in the South has been supported by two conditions:

1. Acceptance of the rationale for it. Segregated schools represent a working compromise between the aspirations of Negroes and the expectations of the oligarchy. Some education, any kind, was regarded by Negroes as giving them needed equipment to advance, however short that advance might be. As a politically powerless people they could take what they must accept and strain the limits set about it. The oligarchy wanted them to have enough learning to give them the maximum efficiency in the roles they were to play in the station in life it had set as their bounds.

2. Development of a structure for maintaining segregated schools. The educational policies for the schools for Negroes were not determined by them but by the oligarchy. The oligarchy could easily enforce its policies for the Negro school by controlling its budget and appointing its administrators and teachers. The oligarchy was able to make the roles of school administrator and school teacher prestige statuses within the Negro group. This prestige was necessary to secure the co-operation and acceptance by Negroes of the school and what it taught.

So the pattern of segregation in the schools came to be fixed.

Policy-making was invested in a school board elected by a restricted electorate responsible to those who voted for them. The members of the school board were white persons who were acceptable to the oligarchy, and the policies they made and enforced must be acceptable. The top administrative official, the school superintendent, whether elected or appointed, must be a white person of proved orthodoxy in his social viewpoint before his professional qualifications were given consideration. Some supervisory positions and the principalships of Negro schools were given to Negroes. These posts and those of the teachers in the Negro schools were to be occupied by persons appointed and approved by the superintendent and the school board. They were required to be amenable to the requirements of the school board and have the ability to gain the acceptance of the Negro community for the playing of their roles.

When the mechanism of segregation of the schools is assembled and in working order the condition for withholding knowledge has been satisfied. The evidence of its handicapping Negroes and its operation to the disadvantage of the nation is overwhelming. In the first place it makes possible uneven distribution of school funds and the educational commodities that those funds purchase: school buildings and equipment, teachers, courses. Whatever rationalization for differentials is accepted, the concession is made that Negroes don't need the education given to white children and it costs less to provide for them. For the school term 1949-50 there were the following differentials in 'Current Expenditures Per Pupil in Average Daily Attendance':

State	White	Negro
Alabama	$144.38	$ 80.76
Florida	185.89	131.32
Georgia	131.67	70.99
Mississippi	119.09	27.45
North Carolina	153.00	113.00

One answer to the question why Negroes want their children to attend the same schools as white children appears here, since it would be impossible to differentiate in the monies apportioned except in the circumstances of segregation.

From the funds allocated for his education, what can the Negro child expect in instruction? The principle underlying educational policy governing the offerings in the Negro school has been *Education for Present Opportunity*. This was interpreted as education for the community in which the child lived. It was described as preparing for a fuller and more constructive life where you live by being able to perform efficiently what you may expect to do in life. This was regarded as practical education and demonstrations of it were applauded. Spokesmen for the white community had high praise for the offerings in home economics, trades and agriculture. An example of how this works in meeting the aspirations of the Negro, and at the same time meeting the expectations of the oligarchy, is given in the following incident.

The principal of a Negro school felt that the girls should be taught home economics so as to teach them how to live better in their homes, be able to sew their own clothing and prepare meals that would supply a more balanced and appetizing diet for themselves and their children.

The school had no facilities for giving such instruction. The principal decided to take some of the money the school had in a small fund that had accumulated from the teachers selling candy and rent a couple of sewing machines. Out of these funds he also decided to employ for a couple of months a competent seamstress for three afternoons a week.

High-school girls who were financially able to buy yard goods and thread were to be given time out of their classes to have the instruction of the seamstress in making simple garments.

At the commencement exercises for that school year the principal succeeded in having an invited group of influential white people present. As a part of the programme the girls marched across the stage wearing the garments that they had made.

This performance succeeded in convincing the school board that it should appropriate money to match federal funds

under a provision called the Smith-Hughes Act. A small
building was erected on the school grounds and some equipment was put in it. A home economics teacher was employed
but poorly paid in a salary scale that was poor.

Nearing the end of the first year of this home economics
instruction, the principal arranged to have the members of
the school board and representatives of the chamber of
commerce come to a dinner prepared for them at the school.
The food prepared and served by the girls made a great
impression on their guests.

At the next meeting of the school board the home economics
teacher's salary was raised—above that of the principal, to
become the highest-paid teacher in the school.

It was not uncommon for the home economics, trades, and
agriculture teachers to draw the highest salaries paid to Negro
teachers. The principal often found it to his advantage to
double as trades or agriculture teacher.

The Negro principal of the segregated Negro school deserves
credit that he seldom receives. Diplomacy and machinations were
required of him in order to improve the offerings in his school.
His first task was to sell influential white persons and his school
board the idea that the white employer and the community at
large would benefit from additional funds put into new offerings
to Negro children. His major task, before that of administering
the school became that of maintaining good public relations for
the school. When he wanted to develop a band or an athletic
team he exploited local pride. His appeal for support of such
activities, stripped of double talk, was that the good white people
of Sandusky couldn't afford to let those of neighbouring Bell-
town provide better for their Negro school.

Another principle that had a strange appeal for support came
in the motto, 'Take what you have and make what you want.'
This amounted to Negro children taking nothing and making
something out of it. In trades and home economics classes
orange crates were made into kitchen cabinets, potato sacks
were made into rugs, and animal feed sacks were made into
dresses. Used tin cans were made into drinking cups, biscuit

cutters, or metal scoops. These creations were produced in the courses that were offered under the title, 'Resource Use Education'. The Negro child came to see that the resources of the community available to him were to be found in the refuse heap.

What the Negro child had learned when he completed high school, or stopped at any point below high school graduation, was certainly not the same thing that the white child at the allegedly comparable level had learned. The same is true of instruction at the college level in tax-supported institutions. Examination of the catalogues of instruction offered in the state colleges show immediately that there is no intent or attempt to provide for Negroes what is provided for white young people.

In the segregated system not all of the institutions to offer instruction to white youths exist for Negroes. In most states of the South the system of higher education includes a university, an agricultural and mechanical college, a technological institute, a medical school, and several teachers colleges for white students. Until two decades ago there was only one institution of higher learning for Negroes supported by public funds. This, under various names, was the Negro agricultural and mechanical college which also incorporated teacher training. Within the last two decades one or more state teachers colleges were added for Negro students. In the last decade, as Negroes came to press for the same instruction as white students and the Supreme Court ordered this to be provided, some of the states have admitted Negroes to the existing institutions and others have made gestures at upgrading the Negro A. and M. college to encompass a wider variety of offerings. The stark fact remains that, where Negroes are not admitted to the same institutions of higher learning that whites attend, there is much that the white young person may learn that the Negro young person may not. Even in the case of those offerings that appear to be the same in pages of the catalogues of the colleges the content will be found to differ in actual instruction. Painstaking documentation of these facts would only prove tedious while not qualifying them.

More important than impressive specification of differentials in the educational offerings in the schools of the South from

E

the elementary school through the college are the results of those differentials that amount to the withholding of knowledge from Negroes. There are three states in the South in which no Negro has been admitted to a white institution of college level, and it is now thirteen years since the Supreme Court ruled they should be.

Some people outside of the South have a concerned awareness of the price that their communities have had to pay for this withholding. Migration into their communities from the South made them painfully aware of the problems that people of limited education present to a community. In 1949, Carl Weigman, a reporter for the *Chicago Tribune*, made an investigation of what the Negro migrant to Chicago cost the city and Cook County. His findings were given in a series of articles that appeared in the *Tribune* between December 29, 1949 and January 4, 1950. In summary the following were his findings:

'This is not the first great migration to Chicago. Earlier there were waves of Irish, German, Italian, Polish, and other immigrants who sought jobs in Chicago industries, just as the southern Negroes are doing today.

'Many of the earlier migrants tended to segregate themselves in certain areas of the city. There were tensions between the groups, sometimes pitched battles. There are still large sections populated predominantly by Poles, Italians, Czechs, and others among the later groups of foreign immigrants. For them, the segregation is voluntary. They are free at any time to seek homes in more attractive neighbourhoods, and in the second and third generations many of them do so.

'For the Negroes, such freedom of movement has not been possible. They have been pushed together in a relatively small area and their more ambitious and competent members have found it difficult to get better homes and living conditions outside of the area. The result has been overcrowding, great tension within the Negro community, and intense pressure to expand their area.

'One survey of a south-side Negro area showed that 3,580 families plus 646 roomers were living in dwelling units built for 1,127 families. Violations of the building laws are common. Alderman Archibald Carey, an aggressive Negro leader, conceded that the laws were not being enforced and said: "If we enforce the laws people would be living in tents in the streets. On my desk I have a list of ninety-eight families who are occupying deplorable places. One mother with seven children is trying to live in one room."

'Advocates of public housing contend this is the only answer, and have high hopes for the success of the programme to build 40,000 federally financed housing units in Chicago in the next six years. This programme has been delayed by a bitter controversy over sites of the projects.

'Chicago now has ten permanent housing developments with 7,680 dwelling units. Of these, about 60 per cent are occupied by Negroes. Four of the ten projects are occupied entirely by Negroes, four are all white, and two are occupied by both Negroes and whites.

'The cost of supporting and policing Chicago's Negro community is a severe drain on the city's taxpayers. This was conceded by Negro leaders, who predicted that the drain would continue until Negroes have had a chance to live and work under conditions equal to those of white citizens.

'The Illinois Public Aid Commission reported that in November 33,305 persons were on relief in Cook County. Of these, 64 per cent were Negroes, although Negroes make up only about 10 per cent of the county's population.

'Aid to dependent children, which is provided by state and federal funds went to 49,412 persons in 13,999 cases in Cook County in July 1949. Of these cases 78.9 per cent were Negroes.

'Taxpayers also are called upon to bear much of the expense of providing medical care for Negroes. They make up 60 per cent of the 83,000 patients treated annually at the County hospital, which has an operating budget of $4,783,085 a year. Negroes comprise 38 per cent of the patients at the Municipal Tuberculosis Sanitarium.

'Many Negroes go to the County hospital because there is no other place for them. The Chicago-Cook County health survey conducted by the United States Public Health Survey in 1947 showed that a total of only 315 beds are available to Negroes in private hospitals, including 155 beds in Provident hospital, the only Negro medical institution. The report also found that approximately 64 per cent of the Negro population cannot afford to pay the cost of medical care.

'Several studies have been made of the high crime rates among Negroes and of the consequent economic losses and expenses of providing police, courts, and prisons. During the first six months of 1949, the Chicago police department reported that felonies were charged against 3,627 white men and 3,140 Negroes. Convictions on misdemeanor charges included 13,268 white persons and 6,903 Negroes.

'Virgil W. Peterson, operating director of the Chicago Crime Commission, said it was erroneous to conclude from these figures that Negroes, as a race, have more tendency to criminality than white persons. "But there is a connection between high crime rates and bad housing conditions, poor health and sanitation, lack of education, inadequate recreational facilities, and faulty law enforcement," he said.

'Another aspect of Chicago's problem is the burden which the migrants from the South have placed upon the city's schools. To accommodate the newcomers the board of education has been obliged to place twelve schools on double shifts, operating one shift from 8.00 a.m. to noon and another shift from noon to 4.00 p.m. Six of the double-shift schools are in Negro areas, three are in white districts, and three in mixed neighbourhoods.

'Simon Stickgold, chief of the division of special services of the Illinois Public Aid Commission, said the only way to take the poor Negro population off the backs of the taxpayers is to attack the problem logically.

'"White people must be educated to understand that discrimination and segregation are costly," he said. "They mean millions of dollars in taxes to support Negroes who become dependent and millions more for Negroes who become delinquent.

"Both dependency and delinquency are the results of generations of neglect. If Negroes received housing, recreation, education and employment opportunities, millions of dollars would be saved for the taxpayers, and untold benefits to the community would result from the contributions they would ultimately make."'

Documentary evidence such as the foregoing might be assembled for other cities into which there has been an influx of migrants from the South. It is not reckless to anticipate that the cost to other cities should be comparable to that of Chicago. It is reported that in the spring of 1956 Negroes with the same lack of skills and limited education were entering Chicago at the rate of 2,500 per month.

In the summer of 1961 there was a nation-wide controversy over new policies for the welfare and relief programme of Newburgh, a small city in New York state. Negro migrants to the city increased 151 per cent between 1950 and 1960. This city of 31,000 population had a 1961 budget for relief of $983,000, most of which was paid to poor, ill-trained and poorly educated Negroes from the deep South. A new city manager drew up, and put into effect, a thirteen-point code:

'A three-month limitation on relief payments, except for the physically handicapped and the aged; unmarried mothers who bore any more illegitimate children would be cut off from assistance; whenever possible, food and rent vouchers would be issued instead of cash; able-bodied males on relief would have to work forty hours each week for the city building-maintenance department; newcomers who settled in Newburgh without specific job offers would be limited to one week of relief payments.'

The premise on which the education of the Negro in the South was predicated was a false one. To educate for present opportunity as the South did in the case of the Negro is to deny one of the obvious characteristics of the American people: they move. This mobility is both geographic and upward in the economic and social scale. As a matter of fact, geographic mobility is largely a function of vertical mobility —people move from one place to another in search of the opportunity to improve their employment, their incomes, and the advantages they might enjoy. The Southern school authorities may not be excused on the grounds of simple short-sightedness in the emphasis they have given the education of Negroes.

Rather than shortsightedness, the school authorities in the South have been guilty of deliberate, purposive withholding. Educational policies were related to the conception of the Negro as the supplier of agricultural labour and domestic service. The concern for a labourer who could efficiently perform the tasks that agriculture and domestic service required assumed and desired that the Negro remain in the South and keep to the station prescribed for him there. With the mechanization of agriculture and the general distribution of labour-saving devices in homes, those traditional skills for which Negroes were valued become obsolete. More and more workers with only these crude skills and the knowledge essential to their efficient use are losing the security they knew in the old system. However disadvantaged their station was it represented a security. This newly-come dispensability encourages the movement of greater numbers to communities outside of the South. Some members of the oligarchy are urging that this movement be accelerated. So the nation may be concerned about the pressure to be put on its resources to adapt such an ill-prepared population to work and live outside of the South. This involves a total community integration that passes a problem, of the South's making, to others for solution.

Total integration makes it necessary that new-comers learn how to use the resources of the community. Many of these migrants simply do not know that facilities for preventive medicine, for pre-natal care, employment services, free public instruction for adults, and many more are available to them in the cities to which they move. Where they come from some of the facilities did not exist and those that were maintained were not open to their use. Their very quest for opportunity is impeded by the lack of knowledge of what is available for their use.

Another effective withholding that segregated schools accomplish is the psychological blockage of the development of co-operative human relations. In the circumstances of separation suspicion and mistrust may be inculcated if positive antipathies are not strengthened or developed. The fruits of this instruction may be observed in many areas of community living within and outside the South. There is greater difficulty in advancing a spirit of antagonism between groups when they are in communication and co-operation in the classroom during the formative years. Sectarianism, or an exclusive belief system, requires isolation for its maintenance. Historically, the believers in an exclusive ideology have withdrawn from those who hold contrary beliefs. In the modern world this form of isolation has become more and more difficult to attain. Instead, psychological isolation has been demonstrated to be as effective as removal in space. Without withdrawing, the sectarian may be emotionally insulated against ideas and beliefs that threaten his own. His beliefs are fixed with such strong emotional overtones that he becomes an evangelist among the present heathen rather than seeking to escape from them.

Segregated schools in the South have permitted emphasis being placed upon difference and imputing to that difference an inferiority-superiority demarcation. In segregated schools white and Negro children are taught the differences in their stations in life. Much of the instruction is through the contrived circumstances, but there is some formal instruction to provide a rationale for these circumstances.

In one Southern small town the class hours of the Negro and white schools were different so as to permit Negro and white children to go to and from school without meeting en route. The Negro school opened and closed half an hour earlier than did the white school. Still some groups of children managed to pass each other and on occasion to pause and do battle. The Negro principal would be informed of his pupils being involved in such an altercation, with the reminder that he was expected to ensure that they would not repeat the transgression. One principal, carrying out his responsibility for preserving the peace, spoke to his pupils along the following lines:

Some of you were fighting with white children yesterday afternoon on Taylor Street. Now we can't have that. You've got to learn to get along with people. When you don't have a show the best thing to do is to avoid the chance of trouble starting. There is no sense in inviting it when you don't stand a chance to win. This is the white man's country. He makes the laws. He has the power. You can't buck him. You haven't got anything to buck him with.

When you meet a disagreeable person on the sidewalk and he tries to hog it all: give it to him. Step off the sidewalk. Get out in the street if you have to. But don't get into a brawl with him when it's pretty sure you are going to be the one to suffer. That may not sound right to you now. I don't say it's right but you will learn that in the long run it's the better thing to do.

You students who go home by Taylor Street have plenty of time to get home before the white school lets out. I want you to go on home and not dawdle along. Your parents are waiting for you at home. They have chores for you to do. Dawdling and clowning in the street is a bad habit. It doesn't become you and it's a reflection on your school. People will say that's what we teach you down here.

Now you children, you that go through Taylor Street and the rest of you: go on home when you leave school. If there's any more of this kind of thing some of you are going to be sorry. I know your parents will not approve of you getting into fights. You know that if I have to punish you here at school you'll get another whipping when you get home.

Many Negro children in the South are familiar with this kind of admonition.

The psychological problems of children who enter the integrated school situation after a period of separation are familiar. Communication and uninhibited responses to each other are difficult when Negro and white children come together after the ages of eight or ten when prior to these ages they have been aware of the separation and have been given some rationale for the circumstance of separation. This may well be anticipated in the South and the nature of the problems may be predicted on the basis of experiences outside of the South.

In those circumstances where segregation has been maintained within or outside the South, removing the bars in the schools makes immediately apparent the damage to human relations that has already been accomplished. Young people who are strangers to each other meet with curiosity and childhood's own devices of introduction—perhaps challenging and sparring before acceptance and the mutual definition by each of the roles of the other and the future relationship prescribed by that definition. Add to this the indoctrination each child has been given about the class of human the individual he encounters represents and you have a clumsy problem created.

White children whose parents and previous experience dispose them to friendliness, experience some frustration and disappointment when Negro children keep apart from them and herd together on the playground and in the cafeteria. A frequently heard question from such a white child is, ' Why do they segregate themselves? '

Those Negro children in a non-segregated school who move together, apart from other children, demonstrate an unfortunate cost of segregation. Shy, awkward, now that they have been included but hardly daring to hope for acceptance, the pangs they know are something they may not be sufficiently articulate to communicate.

Children may not be expected to and adults may not think of the emotional scars these children already bear when they come to a non-segregated school. Sometimes calluses over their bruises and the keloid scar tissue in their spirits may show in bumptiousness or meanness. Privy to these children may be an early consciousness of inadequacy that comes from backwardness for their ages. There may be a straining to keep up with white children in their studies because they have not been given the same instruction up to the point of integration. The limitations of their parents, who are products of the segregated school or

E*

have little education at all, have failed to give them the experiences in the home that makes it possible for them to communicate easily with white children of a different home background.

It is not at all surprising, and certainly nothing to condemn, that white children should find the Negro children different and experience difficulty in establishing a basis of communication and co-operation. It is perfectly natural that the characteristically unvarnished reactions of junior high school and high-school children should be expressed in this relationship as in any other.

If the segregated situation is not to continue, the pain and problems must be endured by some generation. The generation called to make the adjustment that previous ones avoided will be called upon to pay in the coin of emotional stress of varying intensity.

Some of the universities and colleges of the South have now had inter-racial student bodies for almost a decade. Until the incident at the University of Alabama, from none of these campuses had there been reported any serious untoward incident involving Negro and white students. In the light of predictions that adults repeated, that these campuses would become battlegrounds when Negro students appeared on them, it is not surprising that there should be a disturbance at the University of Alabama. The surprising thing is that it did not occur on any of a score of several other campuses at some time during this decade.

There should be no discounting or casually dismissing the experience the college student is having. The ordinary generations' tension and conflict between youth and parent is intensified by the disparity of their race relations opinions. One white student remarked, 'I can't understand it: my Mother and Father are the sweetest people but they are so prejudiced against Negroes. I just can't understand it.' At the fireside and across the dinner table the white college student can't understand his parents, and parents can't understand their children.

Over-simplification of the student's problems should be avoided. Both, Negro and white students, have to face up to the social structure of the college community and its tradition. It is not easy for those students who assume the initiative in doing this. The college community is not homogeneous or lacking in social differentiation. There are fraternities, sororities, residence halls, clubs, and a variety of organized groups that claim distinction on the basis of what students they recruit to memberships and what students they exclude. Where the local campus group is an affiliate of a national organization, it is limited by the national constitution in its choice of members. Even outside of the South there has been controversy over the inclusion of Negroes in the membership of 'local chapters'.

The white students who press for the inclusion of Negroes in their membership groups on a campus do so at the risk of social disapproval. The Negro student who becomes a 'first' in one of these groups must have more than ordinary courage. It requires some courage and a great deal of patience for Negro students to do creditable classwork while waiting for full acceptance at the invisible social and organizational barrier. Even the lustily cheered Negro athlete knows the experience. White and Negro students who find social contacts satisfying face the problem of identification as a prestige-lacking group. The white student who becomes an advocate of Negro acceptance in non-academic activities of the college campus risks dismissal by his fellows as a crackpot or social deviate. Administration and faculty are sometimes resigned to giving the legal inch but are not committed to taking the social ell where the Negro student is concerned.

Despite these problems, on the college campuses of the South and graduating yearly now is a new generation, thinking and acting differently from the many student generations that have preceded them. This development is not without its price.

The result of indoctrination with inferiority-superiority sentiments is the loosing into the society of Negroes and whites who cannot co-operate except in a superordinate-subordinate relationship. The whites may insist that they will not work on a job unless Negro workers are assigned to different tasks which are lower in prestige and pay than those performed by whites. Outside of the South these sentiments have proved to be a headache to personnel directors of plants and have served to confine Negroes to less-skilled poorer-paid jobs. Whites who are schooled in the belief of Negroes' inaptitude and inferiority keep these beliefs, or use them when it is to their advantage in competition for jobs.

Businesses and agencies outside of the South report some disappointing experiences in their efforts to employ Negroes who fail to make full adjustment. They may be efficient workers and satisfactory employees in so far as performance of their duties go. However, as one employer stated his disappointment.

> 'She's a good secretary. She works all right. But one thing I don't like: she hasn't been out to eat her lunch for the six months she's been here. Just sits there and eats a sandwich at her desk. That's not good. I don't know what to do about it. I want to tell her she can eat anywhere in this neighbourhood but maybe she's got other problems like saving her money. I don't want to embarrass her. Some of the girls have invited her to go with them to lunch, but she always excuses herself.'

This sort of psychological problem comes from the insecurity instilled in the South. A worker in this position sometimes feels that any difficulty in the neighbourhood cafes could jeopardize the job she values. Sometimes she has memories of rebuffs in such establishments and does not choose to run the risk of possible unpleasantness. She may consider herself as saving her fellow workers embarrassment. She appreciates their friendly overtures and certainly thinks too well of them to put them in a position that may prove to be an unhappy experience. This complex behaviour is too often dismissed with the assumption that the worker just 'wants to be with her own people'.

Another problem of this sort may also be traced to the lack of learning the social graces and an imperfect comprehension of what integration means. An incident reported by a Negro worker illustrates this:

> 'This new fellow came on the job and the boss was careful to tell him all facilities were open to him. I have been there

years and the other coloured workers know how straight this company is on the race question.

'Well, this fellow's been there three or four days and he comes in the cafeteria and took his tray right over to a table where three white girls in the office always eat together. He didn't even ask to join them. He just plopped down in the empty chair. The girls got up and moved.

'Now, he didn't have to sit in that chair. Plenty of tables were empty. He's just dumb. He doesn't have enough sense to know that you just don't break in on a party of friends like that. He just don't know his manners or what integration means, either.'

Many instances may be reported to illustrate psychological disabilities and distortions that those previously excluded show in the first experience of inclusion. The South has sown the wind by broadcasting the seeds of ignorance of human relations and social skills. Many whirlwinds of personal and social friction are the harvest outside of the South.

Negroes who are indoctrinated with the belief in their own inadequacy and dependence, if not inferiority, present a problem of adjustment. Any white face becomes that of the persecutor. The friendly disposed white person may be alienated by the Negro's responses to whiteness developed over the childhood years. Outside of the South this resentment may take some form of aggression that was denied in the South. Outside of the South, Negroes in the lower economic positions help in the preservation of the ghettos because of the deep feeling of needing to band together for protection, or simply in a desire to be removed from those they feel will use them ill. Many others remain in the ghetto because of devices on the part of whites to confine them there. To seek refuge in the ghetto is the other side of the coin of segregation outside of the South.

Bad government in the South places a premium on bad government outside of the South. Negroes are not unlike other immigrant groups in the issues that become dear to them and the officials they support in terms of these issues. Study of big city political machines that have flourished, dominated by the political boss has come from the partly assimilated recent immigrants. This support is given despite the fact that objective consideration of the machine's policies shows them to be contrary to the interests of the newly-come voter. Call them naïve and gullible and prove it beyond doubt. Yet the fact remains that they are loyal to those declarations with which they identify emotionally. This identification is based on issues related to the homeland and not to the new home.

Like other immigrants the Negroes who move outside of the South are those people who in the homeland were the political underdog and in that position developed astigmatism in viewing government and citizenship. To their own disadvantage these people so conduct themselves politically as to draw antagonism to themselves from other people who are impatient with their support of bad government. An illustration of the appeal made to their loyalty may give some insight into the political price of knowledge and understanding withheld. Mayor William Hale Thompson of Chicago is recognized in history as not having provided that city with its most enlightened administration. Despite the charges against him he secured and held the support of the South Side Negro vote. One of his speeches to a Negro audience from which the following excerpt is taken, suggests the basis of his Negro support:

'Your enemies and my enemies are calling City Hall "Uncle Tom's Cabin". If the Polacks support me it will be Polack Cabin. If the Dagoes support me it will be Dago Cabin. As long as the Negroes of the South Side support me City Hall is going to be Uncle Tom's Cabin.'

Assured of municipal jobs for Negroes and feeling that they had a friend in power, Negroes voted for Mayor Thompson and his organization. All of the virtues of a clean upstanding political figure have little appeal to Negroes when his one blemish happens to be the interests they are most concerned about—the welfare of themselves and those they have left behind in disadvantage. To them their well-being is the paramount consideration; in the South they knew government by men, of whatever virtue, who did not count them as men among men. These politicians used political office and control of education to deprive them of whose skills and that knowledge that would have let them walk in stride with other men.

Those areas outside of the South into which the products of segregated schools are moving must now, and in the future will have to, foot the bill for the knowledge the South withheld from Negroes. The cost will be paid in hard cash appropriated for crime control, economic dependency, health care services, and remedial classes in the schools. This is not the only coin in which these communities must pay. The unadjusted personalities will present problems of social health and community well-being. The politically manipulated will confuse the very process of government. The South will defend its right to conduct its schools in its own way and ask the support of the nation outside of the South for its way, regardless of the price being paid and to be paid.

The governments of the states in the South, these governments alone, are responsible for the kind of education provided to the young in those states. Misuses of their educational responsibilities have been flagrant and insolent. Members of the oligarchy who serve as the spokesmen for these governments are unrepentant for their crimes against generations who in their childhood and youth were so crippled as to arrive at adulthood unfitted for productive and creative lives. The stereotyped self-righteous defences offered by the oligarchy for its indefensible social injustices have become monotonous. The limited usefulness of thousands of soldiers and more thousands of industrial workers is too great a price to pay for the principle of States' rights when one of those rights is consistently abused so as to become a licence to limit the potential of men and women by withholding knowledge from them. Hundreds of thousands of citizens in a status of dependency, that requires taxing of their neighbours for their care, is too dear a price to pay for sympathy and tolerance for the foibles and fancies of a political elite. Domestic political peace is purchased too dearly when its price is the psychological disability of thousands of individuals, as well as group tensions and conflict. The oligarchy and the educational system it manipulates have already levied tribute from the rest of the nation for its educational deeds and misdeeds. The states and communities outside of the South will pay this tribute so long as they condone the freedom of the oligarchy to withhold the knowledge and skills essential to economic independence and responsible citizenship.

CHAPTER X

Modifying Status Patterns

Prejudices against the Negro in the South were, and are still, prejudices in favour of an order that is changing or no longer exists. . . . As far as the South is concerned, it is where racial prejudices, and the social order which they perpetrated, are breaking down, that social animosities are most intense. It is where the Negro invades a new region that race riots occur; it is when he seeks a place in a new occupation or a new profession that he meets the most vigorous opposition; it is when he seeks to assume a new dignity that he ceases to be quaint and becomes ridiculous. . . . The resulting struggle and conflicts (as the effect of the gradual dissolution of the traditional social order) with the incidental disorganization, released all the latent animosities in the old social order, and created antipathies and prejudices between races which previously did not exist. ROBERT E. PARK. 'The Bases of Race Prejudice' in *Annals of the American Academy of Political and Social Science*, volume cxxxx, November 1928, *The American Negro*.

A WHITE man, observing a student demonstration in a Southern city, made the remark that, ' we educate them and see what they do'. A person who was so perceptive should have been wise enough not to be disappointed that these young people should express dissatisfaction with a status defined for the Negro long ago. Since that definition was made the changes that have taken place in the American social order have included the Negro population.

Prediction in 1940 forecast change in the general Negro status in spite of its being 'preserved by legal sanctions'. The greatest change since that time has been the redefinition of the Negro's legal status in the South through a succession of judicial decisions that progressed from removal of specific negative legal sanctions to a positive affirmation of legal protection of common opportunity for Americans without distinction. With the removal of each legal prohibition all sorts of actions for change were initiated. Sight should not be lost of the fact that there were broad economic and social changes that made legal changes not only feasible but urgent.

The changes in population concentration from rural to urban communities are basically significant. The cities in which student demonstrations took place in 1960 and 1961 were those in which there had been substantial population increases between 1950 and 1960, except for Orangeburg, South Carolina. Tallahassee, Florida had the greatest increase in the decade, 76.9 per cent; the Atlanta, Georgia population increased more than 50 per cent; Greensboro, North Carolina 47.9 per cent. The cities had increases in the number of Negroes in the population but Negroes formed smaller percentages of the population in 1960 than they had in 1960. The trend toward urbanization that was so greatly accelerated in the 1940-50 decades appears to have been continued between 1950 and 1960, even though detailed reports of the 1960 census of population are not yet released to make comparisons possible.

Within the South urbanization has greatly accelerated since World War II. In the decade of the 1940's the increase in urban population was 39 per cent in the South as compared to 15 per cent for the non-South. The increase in the urban Negro population (26 per cent) was smaller than that of the white population (43 per cent). More white people in the South moved within the region, while the greater movement of Negroes was out of the region. Migration within the South showed a higher proportion of Negroes going into the central cities than of whites who moved into metropolitan areas. The rural areas and the small market towns of the South continue to be strongholds of that Southern tradition which is least yielding to change in the Negro's status. However, population reduction in such areas is making them less important economically and politically.

All this change of residence appears to be opportunity-related. For the most part it may be considered as positive action. Individuals and families go from where they are to reported opportunities so as to realize some hope or aspiration. There are people who do not aspire to leave the rural area but who encounter experiences which make their moving necessary whether desirable or not. Therefore, change of residence continues to be a problem-solving device. Despite some difference of opinion and much rationalization, it appears that the disadvantaged in rural society seek to relieve that disadvantage by moving. Young people entering the labour market, women, Negroes, and the landless, seem to move in greater relative numbers than those who see the possibility of realization of their aspirations where they are.

In 1950, 74 per cent of Southern non-rural Negroes were located in fifty-one major cities. John M. Maclachlan and Joe S. Floyd, Jr., in *This Changing South*, projecting trends of the 1950's, concluded that by 1970 the Southern Negro will be predominantly urban and concentrated heavily in the region's largest metropolitan areas'. Larger cities in the South undertook 'urban redevelopment' measures in the decade of the 1950's. These measures involved clearing away slums in which Negroes had become concentrated in the centre of the cities and replacement of these with new housing planned for higher rent occupancy than the displaced population could pay. This usually means that these became areas of white residence. Planned new housing developments in the South have made for more rather than less segregation. Greater residential segregation of course makes for more segregation in schools and in other institutional services.

While the Negro professional and white-collar workers have increased impressively, the large migration into the cities has placed there an unskilled low-income population for which housing and jobs are acute problems.

Uncomfortable farm homes with only crude conveniences have not been encouraging to the stability of the farm family. The conveniences and comforts of the farm home have been increased by the widespread distribution of electric power. In 1930, 13.4 per cent of American farms had electricity. In 1950, 78.3 per cent reported electric water pumps to provide running water and 58.7 per cent, or 75 per cent of those having electricity reported electric washing machines. Associational and recreational opportunities of the farm family have not been encouraging to its stability. All of these relative disadvantages in the rural community could, in the past, be overcome only by excessive expenditure of energy, time, and money. Even the least privileged in the South show evidences of participating in these changes. The meanest shacks on Southern farms will have some kind of automobile parked outside and over many a television antenna rises.

The economic status of Southern Negroes was greatly improved in 1949 over what it was in 1935-36, despite the fact that it had not improved as much as had the economic status of whites who received favoured employment opportunity. Urban Negro families earning less than $1,000 annually decreased from 90 to 40 per cent in this period. By 1954, the median annual income of urban Negroes in the South was $2,425, which was 56 per cent of the median income of urban whites. The median incomes of both rural-farm whites and rural-farm Negroes remained low in 1954, with the $749 median for Negroes being 49 per cent of the median for whites. However, the fact that half of the urban Negro families in the South had an income of more than $2,500 indicates a greatly improved economic status over that suffered by a predominantly rural Negro population two decades earlier. Increasing recognition of the importance of the Negro market to the economic well-being of the region causes Negroes themselves to have consciousnss of the economic power it gives them and relates directly to the use of the boycott as pressure for fuller participation in the society.

Students of the Southern scene have documented, statistically, the changes in the South over the past two decades. Their conclusions are in agreement with those of John M. Maclachlan and Joe S. Floyd, Jr., in *This Changing South*: 'strain towards consistency with national levels of economic performance' accompanied by cultural changes as aspects of the same fundamental trend. Trends in the status of Negro Southerners indicate the same strain with especially aggressive action to remove invidious distinctions in their citizenship status. The result is a vitally dynamic conception of their citizenship role on the part of Negroes. Professor William G. Carleton, writing on the South in the summer 1958 issue of the *Antioch Review*, expressed the

view that these changes have improved the Negro status:
'Groups once underprivileged and exploited are no longer under-
privileged and can no longer be exploited as they were. With
rising living standards and educational advantages members
of once-exploited groups have come to have more respect for
themselves and are getting more respect from others.'

From Emancipation to the end of the nineteenth century,
Negroes in the South occupied a great diversity of prestige positions. Whites who had been excluded from the richer areas of
the South during slavery began moving into these areas immediately following the Civil War. The economic advancement
of these poor whites depended upon successful competition for
the better-paid occupations followed by Negroes. Already in
the South were those middle-class whites who had been agents
and functionaries of the aristocracy, or who provided the goods
and services the plantation economy required. Upward mobility
of the whites required that the upper-middle class encroach upon
the upper class, the lower-middle class move upward, and the
lower class enter the middle class, by competing with Negroes
who occupied economic positions superior to their own.

Negroes, who had a near monopoly on the building trades, gave
way before white artisans who showed determination to preempt
these lucrative occupations. There were those genteel service
occupations regarded as 'Negro jobs' to which there was
attached considerable prestige—barbers, caterers, and operators
of livery services were in this category. Ambitious and aggressive
whites soon took over these pursuits. By the end of the century
the Negro holder of public office and the political leader had
been replaced by whites whose educational level and manners
compared unfavourably with those of their Negro predecessors.
Negro organized and operated business establishments first ex-
perienced limitation to Negro patronage, followed by competition with whites for this patronage. The second decade of the
twentieth century found the ministry and teaching to be the
only professions followed by Negroes in significant numbers.

By 1930, the range of prestige occupations for Negroes in the
South had narrowed and some of these categories were sparsely
populated, indeed. Negroes in the professions and other high-
status occupations accompanied or followed the masses of Negro

workers who migrated to the North during World War I. Following this war middle-class whites mobilized lower-class whites into the phalanxes of the Ku Klux Klan, whose programme included neutralizing, if not destroying, the influence of upper-class whites along with repression and subordination of Negroes. The 'nigger lover', who scorned his own colour because it was not his kind, shared the animosity of the striving whites with the 'uppity nigger' who had to be taught his place. At the height of the Ku Klux Klan activity. Success, affluence and dignity were dangerous attributes for Negroes to possess and subjected their possessors to insult, if not injury. Perhaps at no time in his history had a Negro who occupied a prestige position been so insecure and subjected to intimidation as he was in the decade following World War I.

Sanford Winston's study, 'The Migration and Distribution of Negro Leaders in the United States', reporting on Negroes in the 1928-29 edition of *Who's Who in Coloured America*, showed that 77 per cent of Negro 'leaders' were born in the South, but only 40 per cent of these lived in the South. Charles S. Johnson, in *The Negro College Graduate*, reported that only 18 per cent of Negro college graduates born in the South had migrated. It should be noted that 62 per cent of Negro college graduates at this time were teachers whose opportunity for employment was in the South.

It is noted above that nearly two-thirds of Negro college graduates were teachers of some sort. Physicians, surgeons, and dentists ranked second to teachers, being 8 per cent of Negro college graduates. Ministers were a close third (7.9 per cent) and lawyers were fourth as 2 per cent. The college-trained did not occupy all prestige positions among Negroes, but all of them had prepared for occupations that were expected to give them prestige.

In the smaller places in the South, prestige positions in the Negro community were occupied by the Negro professional, the occasional successful business man, and the property-owning servitor of upper-class whites. These leading Negroes, by virtue of their sponsorship, could not escape demands put on them for leadership. They were intermediaries who interpreted whites to Negroes and Negroes to whites and who, because of their influence, enjoyed consideration if not respect from both whites and Negroes.

White prestige positions have not depended upon relationships with Negroes, but historical circumstance has made paternalistic sentiment an attribute of aristocratic and upper-class white status. Their sponsorship of their mulatto offspring and their servants extended itself to a generalized encouragement of Negro aspirations to economic and social advancement. They were considered as the Negro's protectors from the aggression of 'poor whites' against Negroes. John Dollard, in *Caste and Class in a Southern Town*, reported that the only protestors against white solidarity and the current treatment of the Negro he encountered were upper-class people. The attitudes and sentiment of the upper-class white person toward Negroes have influenced his position in the southern community. Dollard observed that the upward mobility of middle-class whites as they have risen from lower-class positions involved aggression against upper-class whites with rejection and attack on the assistance given Negro upward mobility by upper-class whites.

White middle-class people have 'vigorous hostile attitudes toward the Negroes and are seldom found in the ranks of those who take the friendly attitude toward the Negro evinced by the white aristocracy'. It is not uncommon for the middle-class white with his own limited resources to undertake the sponsorship of Negroes. However, this sponsorship is for definitely restricted aspirations and cannot be distinguished from subordination for crudely disguised exploitation. In *Deep South*, Allison Davis and Burleigh Gardner commented that in this group of southern whites, 'ability to subordinate Negroes is for some positions a prime requisite and such a reputation a political asset'. The middle-class whites in the South consider their continued mobility as depending upon aggression against the upper class, one of whose vulnerabilities is 'softness' on the subject of Negro upward mobility. Racial solidarity becomes a key to their aspirations if the lower-class whites recognize Negroes as competitors who are given an advantage by upper-class subordination of Negroes, for which the neutralizing of upper-class whites is essential.

The student demonstrations in the South have been very

largely a Negro middle-class expression. That most of these demonstrations occurred in cities where colleges are located is not a coincidence. In these cities there is a relatively large Negro middle-class group, while the colleges themselves must be recognized as the matrix of the middle class because the students are seeking the education that will give them access to occupations and incomes that identify the middle class. Before the students engaged in their demonstrations there had been legal action to desegregate public schools, transportation facilities and public recreation.

The controversy over desegregation in the South, with its promise of far-reaching changes in the traditional pattern of race relations, is already having its influence on intra-racial status and prestige positions. The shift in statuses and prestige positions has been more pronounced in those areas where resistance to desegregation has been adamant than where some desegregation is an indication of the strength of the established leadership of the white portion of the community, and acceptance of the method and pace of desegregation is an indication of the strength of the established Negro leadership. The prestige of this white and Negro leadership is preserved by their maintaining communication and following a course of action that is generally opposed by the radical element in each racial group.

In the areas of implacable resistance to desegregation traditional communication practices have been disturbed and in crisis situations this communication has ceased. Cessation of communication indicates that the status positions of these whites and Negroes are in jeopardy. Loyalties that obtained across the race line have been undermined. In crisis situations prestige among whites and among Negroes has shifted from a basis of economic status and social position to devotion and service to the cause of segregation or of desegregation. Racial solidarity has been made the primary value with leaders of *the cause* within each group, who are taking prestige positions formerly held by leading citizens whose prestige positions were based upon other than identification with a racial cause. Economic security and social approval come to depend upon adherence to the cause as it is defined by the leadership seeking to maintain segregation or advance desegregation. Community tension and crisis over desegregation brings into sharp focus the inter-dependence of intra-racial statuses and relationships across the race line.

Negroes who occupy prestige positions are generally lumped together as 'Negro leaders'. In considering status changes, a useful dichotomy may be made by distinguishing between 'leading Negroes' and 'Negro Leaders'. The leading Negroes of any community may be readily identified on a pretty objective basis. According to standards of the communities in which they live, these are distinguished or well-respected persons. According to prevailing standards they are economically secure, follow occupations that carry prestige, and fill roles to which honour is attached in the community. These are Negroes of advanced achievement and economic status, who demonstrate Negro opportunities and set aspiration goals for the ambitious. In the past they may have avoided controversy and have had their prestige rest on respect given them by both whites and Negroes for service to the community. Among them, however, the 'conservative' Negro leadership is to be found.

In rural areas, and smaller urban places in the deep South, the behaviour of the conservative leadership is suggested in one characterization of upper- and middle-class Negroes by Davis and Gardner: 'The Negro upper and middle classes do not support any local associations or movements designed to disrupt the separate endogamous system of organizing Negro-white relations.' Drawn from these classes, the Negro conservative leader identifies the Negro's cause with the consideration of the white ruling class. His counsel usually includes the contention that Negro demonstration of worthiness will elicit white sponsor-ship and steadily, if slowly, advance potential goals to which Negroes may acceptably aspire. Oliver C. Cox says of the situation:

'The ruling class, possessing the power, is able to endow the conservative leader with sufficient vicarious authority and control of material things to make it obvious to the people that his way is the correct one and that those who oppose him, because of the material emptiness of their leadership, are utopian dreamers.'

The conservative Negro leader is convinced, and sometimes convincing, that his devotion to the Negro's cause is unquestionable, and his method of serving it is sound and reasonable. He is a leader, one committed ideologically to advancement of the Negro's cause, the categoric 'race man'.

Contesting the leadership of the conservative is that other 'race man' called Cox 'the protest leader'. This leader, in contrast to the conservative, enjoys little if any white sponsorship in the local community. While the conservative leader avoids the antagonism of the white middle class by bringing to bear on it the influence of his white sponsorship, the protest leader is in continuous conflict with the middle class and a source of embarrassment to the white upper class upon whom he presses claims for positive action, as expression of personal and class commitment to justice, fair play, and restriction on Negro aspiration and social participation only by reason of education and social fitness.

The Negro protest leader eschews subtle, indirect, and camouflaged measures to advance the Negro's cause. He uses legal, political, economic, and educational measures directly in the struggle for improvement of the Negro's status. This direct action, with its presumption of unconditional rights, its expression of confidence in the unqualified capacity of its representatives to acquit themselves creditably in contest, and its eagerness to play serious economic and political games in accordance with the rules prescribed by whites for their own contests is to middle-class whites unpardonable impertinence. The protest leader rejects the conservative leader's tactics, which involve supplication and prayer for relief of onerous disabilities through informal channels or by enlistment of a white champion to represent the cause in open contest. The protest leader rejects the basic conception of Negro dependence, which the conservative leader uses as an instrument to secure advances as privileges granted by the strong.

Much has been written and said about the 'breakdown of communication' between Negroes and whites in the South. The late Charles S. Johnson observed that communication was not the real issue, but acceptance of an agenda was. The voluntary associations have effectively proscribed communication.

Negroes in prestige positions who would accept the KKK or WCC agendas of white supremacy would be difficult to find. Whites in prestige positions who would be willing to make concessions that accept parts of the Negro agenda are restrained by the pressures of the white voluntary associations. Negroes who would make concessions are likewise constrained not to do so. Informal communication between upper-class whites and upper-class Negroes has been interrupted. Offers to replace this informal communication with negotiations of a formal character have been rejected in most places in the South.

The break between sponsor and sponsored is based on each feeling that the other has failed him. Negroes feel that the sponsor, who has done many things, has failed, by not using his influence to restrain the middle-class whites. This attitude shows lack of understanding that the aggressive middle class has limitation of the upper-class white's influence as an objective. The sponsor also feels that he has been failed when the sponsored conservative does not temper or silence the Negro protest leader. This attitude shows a lack of understanding that the Negro conservative leader had the same objectives as the protest leader despite his different methods. The white sponsor may not remember that the conservative leader must not lose his popularity among Negroes if he expects to influence them in the future.

The apparent common denominator among Negroes and whites is the exacting racial loyalty that takes precedence over any class identification and pride. Negro lower-status persons take considerable satisfaction in having upper-class Negroes share with them the mass meetings. A frequently heard remark is 'we're all just Negroes together, now'. In one city the facetious remark is often repeated that the Negroes should erect a monument to the executive secretary of the White Citizens Councils, for bringing all Negroes into co-operation, which never before had been possible. Whites, too, boast about a newly-come solidarity among them as they seek to counteract Negro oppression.

In the smaller places in the South, the upper-class whites are few and at the mercy of, or allied with, the middle-class whites. In rural areas the planters who have achieved economic supremacy assume the outward show of the landed aristocracy, to which they do not belong, and in moving from middle-class positions in one or two generations they have not acquired the sentiments or accepted the code of the true upper class of which they are ersatz copies. However, they assume sponsorship roles. Their sponsorship carries with it limitations on the aspiration level of those sponsored by them. They remain aloof while the middle class discourages Negroes from raising this aspiration level and move to intervene when this discouragement goes to the extent of depressing the aspiration level they approve.

It is in the behaviour of these powerful individuals that the rudimentary evidence appears of the mode of operation of the upper class in the cities. The upper class, as the true locus of power, does not become involved in operational manœuvres. So long as the conduct of affairs, racial as well as otherwise, comes within policies defined by them they are not involved. When policy formulation is in order their decisions are made known.

In the larger cities of the South direct sponsorship occurred a generation ago and the personal relationship of sponsor and sponsored was interred with them. The prestige enjoyed by the management of large Negro business enterprises no longer depends upon personal sponsorship. Upper-class whites and upper-class Negroes are not in communication. Floyd Hunter's study of a southern city, *Community Power Structure*, reports communication taking place between upper-class whites and middle-class Negroes and between upper-class Negroes and upper-middle-class whites. Upper-class Negroes pride themselves on operating as upper-class whites do, remaining out of operational activities which their agents and representatives conduct satisfactorily. Negro representation in city government in Durham, North Carolina, and desegregation of buses in New Orleans, Louisiana, are attributed to upper-class whites and upper-class Negro 'understandings', but neither appeared among negotiators carrying out the operations that achieved these things.

The sponsor-sponsored relationship which protected Negro advancement for three generations since the Civil War is breaking up. The break-up is taking place in varied forms. Co-operation and collaboration on the basis of common interest—class, profession, labour, etc.,—at its emergence has been stalled by the apartheid policies and pressure-group tactics of the white middle class which, in its desperate stand, is using every appeal to colour antagonism and is exploiting every psychological disposition of those below to aggress against those above.

The latter feature of the middle-class programme appears to be the over-reaching that threatens the success of the whole programme. Huey Long, the prototype of the upwardly straining middle-class personality, boasted that he never won a plurality of votes in a Louisiana town with street cars. Atlanta has four times sought judicial relief from a vote-counting system that gives the smallest rural county in Georgia the same political weight as that of the largest city and its county in the state. The *word* has gone out in several major cities in the South that the middle class and their ' wool hat ' kin who are their source of strength must be stayed. This staying is called for when the middle class enjoys its greatest power from having at its disposal tax revenue supplied by industrial interests undreamed of a decade ago. The middle-class white, and especially his representatives who control state governments in the South, must be stayed, not from obstructing Negro advancement, but from stalling and delaying advancement of the whole people. A new sponsorship appears probable from an upper class and a power group remote from personal relationships with the sponsored. This circumstance suggests a new leadership, one committed to advocacy of a programme for the common good.

A Negro high school principal in Mississippi described his manœuvre as a sponsored Negro leader, in what he considered to be serving the best interests of Negroes and the total community.[1] He heads a public school, newly built, and named for him. His telephoned word to sheriff, judge, or any business man in the town served the Negro for whom he interceded well, indeed. For many years he accepted commissions from his sponsors to take the leadership of the ' Negro division ' of drives of different sorts. Withal, he is a man of no little wisdom. He reports :

' Last year, the Superintendent called me in and told me they

[1] Cox has indicated these conservative leaders were withal leaders and not traitors.

wanted me to be chairman of the United Fund Drive, again. I told him that I wanted the drive to be a success and I would do everything I could to help make it a success. But, I thought my people would support it better if they picked their own chairman. I told him I'd convene the leading coloured men in the community and put it before them, if that was all right with him. He agreed to that.

I got the got men together and explained to them what the score was. They elected their chairman for the drive. They picked a young fellow—a business man who was president of the local NAACP. He did a wonderful job and the Negro division got more money last year than it ever had.'

Many sponsored Negroes lack the perceptive acumen, and certainly the good-humoured acceptance of the shift in prestige among Negroes from the conservative leader.

Leading Negroes, and the conservative leaders among them, may be regarded as serving the Negro population as best they might under circumstances prevailing. However, their achievements sometimes failed to inspire young Negroes, who attribute their success to personal attributes that the aspiring do not possess. The Negro protest leader, like the white middle-class leader, makes a class appeal and often makes capital of the lack of special attributes that provide individual advantage.

The first citizen of Montgomery, Alabama, for many years was Dr H. Council Trenholm, President of Alabama State Teachers College. His interpretation, his intercession, his dogged pushing away of barriers inch by inch, earned for him the respect of Negroes, while his survival as head of a state institution in Alabama attests to respect he had from a half dozen governors and their superintendents of public instruction, as well as many legislatures that provided funds for the institution under his administration. He maintained cordial relations with E. D. Nixon and Rufus Lewis, protest leaders both. As the spokesman for the Negroes in the bus boycott, the renown of young Reverend Martin Luther King, Jr., eclipsed that of other leaders in Montgomery, and in a matter of months he had become spokesman for a positivist philosophy for the Negro minority in the United States that came to be impressed in many places and circumstance in non-violent social action.

Contrasted with the public-relations-wise Reverend King is Professor Charles C. Gomillion, forty miles from Montgomery at Tuskegee. Gomillion is nearly twice Reverend King's age, and is the product of no vagary of fate. He is a 'solid' man, dedicated to the Negro's cause, whose modus of achievement is the vote. For thirty years as a Tuskegee Institute teacher and official, he has urged and prodded people there to register to vote—and to vote. In a characteristic monotone he repeats his message to small groups and to mass meetings where hundreds rise when he enters a church or an auditorium. He respects the conservative leaders who have served the Negro's cause before him. The conservative leaders at Tuskegee admire and envy him. They support him and would abstain from any effort to discredit him or his programme.

In the present era no development commands more attention than the return of Negro ministers and lawyers to leadership positions. The law is no longer the 'starvation occupation' that Charles S. Johnson described it as being in 1932. The success of NAACP lawyers Charles H. Houston and Thurgood Marshall has made of the law again a prestige position as it was before 1900. Z. Alexander Looby in Nashville, Oliver Hill in Richmond, Fred Gray in Montgomery and Arthur Shores in Birmingham are representative of lawyers with prestige who are leaders. They meet and beat the legal talent of the state governments.

Negro ministers have long been in the conservative leadership class. They counselled patience and forbearance on the part of Negroes, to the great satisfaction of the white middle class. Now, the distinguished ministers in the South are those who have taken the protest leadership—Reverends King and Abernathy in Montgomery, Steele in Tallahassee, Shuttlesworth in Birmingham, Borders in Atlanta, with Martin and Buford in Tuskegee, all representative of the new militant ministry. It is significant that the ministers and lawyers, whose professions involve influencing opinions, are the most skilled logicians. They are also in professions in which success depends upon a Negro following. No white sponsor can assure them security, as is possible in some other professions. Yet there remain many Negro preachers who cling to their sponsored relationship and do not join the young ministers in their uncompromising action programmes.

Leaders of protest and positive action include some Negro business men, physicians, dentists, and college professors who place their loyalty to their Negro followers above any relationship with the white power structure. Some of these have to pay penalties of harrassment and economic pressure imposed by the power structure. State and city employees, college and public school teachers are deterred in many places in the South from taking active roles in the organizations and activities for furthering desegregation. Most presidents of local NAACP chapters and other organizations pressing the cause of desegregation are now drawn from those who depend for a livelihood on a Negro clientele and against whom the local whites can take fewer reprisals.

Population changes, expansion of the Negro middle class, emergence of a new leadership among Negroes, adoption of the practice of direct action following legal clarifications of their prerogatives, and new policies of the federal government in the protection of civil rights, together, have effected some improvement in the Negro status in the South. From beginnings made under the chairmanship of Vice President Richard M. Nixon, the President's Committee on Government Contracts has moved to more aggressive action under the chairmanship of Vice President Lyndon B. Johnson. The Commission on Civil Rights, established by the Civil Rights Act of 1957 by the U.S. Congress, after a slow beginning in 1958 has become a force the Southern states must reckon with as the Civil Rights Division of the Department of Justice follows up reports of the Commission with legal action to protect voting rights. The Kennedy administration is placing emphasis on the guarantee of voting rights, with the logic that the vote is the instrument of the citizen to be used in providing local and state governments responsive to the will of the governed.

As an appropriate reminder, attention may be called to the mass of the Negro population that continues to be economically disadvantaged and culturally deprived. They are not committed to non-violent philosophy. Their articulation with the Negro middle-class leadership is poor, and their distrust of white people is strong. They are disadvantaged people who do not understand that *they are a problem; they have problems,* among which is the failure of the powerful and the spokesmen of their own colour group to appreciate the importance of their problems to them.

CHAPTER XI

Another Generation

CIRCUMSTANCES of cultural change over the past quarter of a century have produced new functions, new roles, for both whites and Negroes, with new relationship patterns between them emerging. The many changes that might be described are affecting the young even more than their elders. They are learning and experiencing without the need for unlearning or forgetting. Their normal expectations in many things exceed the vague, fond hopes of their parents' childhood.

Happenings in the South in the past decade have influenced our national political arrangements and affected the national image in the rest of the world. Critical national and international considerations, however, are no more important than the impact of their own experiences on this generation of young Americans.

Children and youth in the past decade have known the impact of an ideological controversy in which there have been massive efforts at persuasion to one or another point of view about the values of this society. The children in the South have had to give heed to passionate indoctrination, directed specifically to them. Their introduction to our social institutions, and especially our political institutions, has been quite different from that given other generations of children. The general and somewhat idealized textbook descriptions may be essentially the same as before, but through the mass media and from interpretations by their elders, institutions which directly affect their daily lives are made to appear quite differently and often far from ideal. The conclusions they reach about the society and government will influence the kind of citizens they become.

The hopes of Negro youth today about their tomorrow are

in striking contrast to the hopes their fathers held. Negroes
below the age of twenty in 1960 know what immediate drastic
change means. They are too sophisticated to discuss a change
affecting them as being fortuitous. They have been shown that
any change in their future means a change, perhaps a disturbing
one, in their present. They can make plans for tomorrow because
something happened yesterday and is happening today. These
children see the names of Bates in Little Rock, Shuttlesworth
in Birmingham, King in Montgomery, Looby in Nashville,
Steele in Tallahassee, et al. in the news receiving recognition
and honours for the challenges they have made of the old
system. These new leaders have eclipsed in stature those who
previously enjoyed prestige in the South. They have heard
about, read about, or seen on television children just like themselves also doing something they could also do. The featuring of
respected Negro adults and courageous Negro children in front-
page news, in contrast to the customary practice of ignoring Negroes (except for criminal acts), the furore over interposition and
massive resistance, and the quickened concern of Southern legislatures over their education, heretofore long neglected, projected
Negro children into a sudden prominence they had never known.
They realize the eyes of the world are on this drama as it unfolds,
with Negro children playing star roles for the first time in their
lives, supported or opposed, as the case may be, by their white
contemporaries, as they make their personal decisions in a new
relationship. This generation of children lives in a climate of
change, whose course it will increasingly influence.

There is a story told of a Negro airman and a white airman
whose cross-country flight brought them near the white airman's Mississippi home, which they proceeded to visit. When
the family was seated, the father could not control himself and
blurted out:

'Well, I never broke bread with a nigger in my life!'
The son reassured him:
'It's all right, Pa. This here fellow's all right. He ain't one
of them old kind of niggers; he's one of them new Negroes.'

Small children who pass through mobs to enter the first grade
in a desegregated public school, high-school pupils and college

students who demonstrate against segregation, and young men in the armed services belong to a generation that is actively making its own future.

It has become obvious that the future of very few Negro children is in the rural South. This means that the belief system belonging to the plantation tradition is obsolete. The rapidity with which it became obsolete leaves many people unaware that it is. One of the ideas that is difficult to accept is that children are no longer a productive asset. In most types of agriculture, particularly in cotton growing, machinery has made the hand labour of children uneconomical. There was the long period of years when schooling was regarded as being of little importance for Negro farm children. Their futures were seen to be in the fields and the more they worked there, the better they could learn what they needed to know to replace their parents. Farmer parents themselves needed the labour of their children to add to their poor incomes and rationalized keeping them at work rather than in school.

This has changed, but there are parents who do not realize the change. An Alabama mother reported with some indignation her inability to have her children employed by the planter for whom her husband worked. Her story as she told it was this:

'I went to Mr —— and asked him to give my children work. You know I got eight children and this undergrowth have to help to take care of itself.

'He told me he didn't have no work for 'em and to send them to school.

'I told him that's what I wanted to do, let them make money to buy things they needed for school cause they didn't have 'em and I couldn't buy 'em.

'He say for me to make out a list of what they need and give it to him. I did and when he went to town he got it and come back and left it on the porch. Then he say he's take so much every week out of my husband's wages to pay for 'em.'

This represents a great change from two decades ago, when every child was recruited to harvest cotton and schools had split terms so that children could help with the harvest. Now the children were not needed and the tractor-driving father was being called on to supply his children with their needs. A study of a Mississippi county showed that as the Negro population declined school enrolment and attendance actually went up. The need for fewer workers caused police officers in the town to check trucks of cotton pickers and remove children under sixteen because they were not needed in the fields.

The greatest opportunity for child workers in the South today is in vegetable and fruit production, which uses migratory workers for brief periods. This problem has been intensely studied during the past decade and there are agencies actively working to do something about the children in migratory families, who follow harvests from Florida to North Carolina, and on out of the South to New York state. These are the most disadvantaged children in the South today. Their experiences threaten to restrict their futures to the transient life of migratory workers.

While in the past decade institutional supports have undermined sanctions for segregation through changes in laws and governmental policies, population movements penetrating the old boundaries with the tensions accompanying this change as well as the shock waves following reversal of the 'separate but equal' concept, have served to strengthen environmental supports for segregation and discrimination. Instead of a welcome to urban centres, Negro migrants are facing a concern over how to stem the tide as city officials and agencies try to grapple with the problems their predecessors had already brought. Notwithstanding the lack of foresight in planning to assimilate these newcomers, who had been on the move increasingly since the outbreak of World War II, the movement continues. Nevertheless, as these Negro children change residence from rural to urban areas, they become beneficiaries of educational opportunities, recreational facilities, and health and welfare services superior to those available to them before.

As the number of man-hours necessary to produce consumer goods is progressively reduced, employment in the future must be sought in types of jobs other than in manufacturing industries. Expanding opportunities are appearing in the service occupations. Already this is being recognized in educational systems that have introduced distributive education at the high-school level. Opportunities in this field for Negro youth are small because traditional thought-forms do not include apprenticeships for young Negroes in business establishments. However, the Negro market is receiving more and more consideration from business management, and increasing opportunities are being provided for young Negroes learning management of service enterprises, especially those which serve predominantly Negro consumers. Gulf Oil, in its training programme and in giving assistance to petrol retailers, has made a notable beginning in providing opportunities for young Negroes. Employment of Negroes on public relations staffs and as sales representatives by large business concerns indicates the serious consideration being given the Negro market. This suggests greater employment opportunities to come.

There is evidence that increasing numbers of young Negroes are looking forward to futures in the South, rather than planning to realize their hopes and dreams outside of the South. Even young Negroes who go outside of the South for their career preparation expect to follow those careers in the South. The development of Negro communities in Durham, Atlanta, Nashville and New Orleans are evidence of this. The improvement of living conditions among all classes in these cities over the past decade shows the confidence that some Negroes have in the future of the South.

Transmission of the culture to the young, both through formal education and informally through the several social devices for preparing them for their functions and roles, is preparation for the future of the society. Education may not prepare the young for the future when the future has not been anticipated with a reasonable degree of realism. Sometimes only a crisis will bring the realization that the education being provided falls short of its intended purpose.

The first real concern, nationally and regionally, about the effective literacy of Negroes came as a result of the rejection rates of Selective Service during World War II. The comparative inferiority of schools for Negroes becomes a consideration in the desegregation of schools, to the end that Southern public officials have undertaken earnest programmes to improve Negro schools even if there is no real intent to make them equal to those of whites. Since 1950 there has been accelerated investment in educational facilities for Negroes, both at the common school and higher-education levels.

Donald J. Bogue, in a paper in *The New South and Higher Education*[1], concluded that 'a rise in the average level of educational attainment was one of the greatest of the recent transformations in the South. The level of educational attainment climbed much faster for the South's non-white population than for the white. The number of non-white Southerners with some high school or college education increased faster than for white Southerners in all geographic divisions.'

In the 1940's the gap between the provision of education for Negroes and whites began to narrow. Current expenditures, school plants and facilities, the length of school term, the training of teachers all showed a marked advance. Pressures brought to bear on the South effected this increase in educational provisions. The threat of desegregation of schools, as the only reliable means by which Negro children could receive the same educational opportunity as white children, caused greater portions of education funds to be allocated to Negro schools in an effort to preserve the segregated system. In the deep South increased funds for Negro schools were continued despite the 1954 Supreme Court decision that signalled the end to separate schools in a not so distant future.

Meanwhile, South Carolina continued with its ambitious programme of school equalization and expansion, financed by a 3 per cent sales tax initiated in 1951. Since 1951 the state has spent or approved for school construction the sum of $174,617,124 —51·4 per cent of this for Negro schools. Initial expenditures under this programme went 75 per cent or better to Negro projects. Negroes make up 42·3 per cent of South Carolina's school population.

Mississippi and other states were moving forward (and still are) with extensive school equalization programmes. The 1955

[1] Jessie P. Guzman, ed.. *The New South and Higher Education* (Tuskegee Institute, Tuskegee, Alabama: The Department of Research and Records, 1954).

Mississippi legislature authorized $120 million for school physical equalization over a period of years. By April 1957 more than $13 million worth of school construction had been authorized by the Educational Finance Commission, 80 per cent of this for Negro buildings. Florida was already ahead of most Southern states in this respect, with a minimum foundation programme which dated back to 1947. In November 1955 *Southern School News* estimated that $2,556,500,000 had been spent or appropriated for new school construction in sixteen states and the District of Columbia since 1949.[1] The June 1959 *Southern School News* reported that a new appropriation to the white-Negro school equalization fund brought the total to $65 million with 70 per cent going to Negro families.

'Despite the significant difference between the average expenditures in the South and the rest of the country, and despite the persistence in most states of much larger expenditures for white than for Negro pupils, the past decade has witnessed a real effort in the South to increase its expenditures for both white and Negro pupils, with particular stress on the latter. For instance, between 1941 and 1951 Alabama increased its expenditures per pupil enrolled about 170 per cent for whites and 530 per cent for Negroes. At the present time the state itself spends the same amount for Negroes as for whites; such differences as remain reflect local funds which account for only 20 per cent of the total. Between 1930-50 Florida increased the total amount spent on white pupils from $62 to $186 and from $17 to $131 for Negroes. During this same period Louisiana increased its expenditures per pupil from $46 to $142 for whites and from $12 to $87 for Negroes. In South Carolina expenditures for white pupils increased from $58 to $113, and for Negroes from $8 to $54. Between 1940 and 1951 Arkansas increased its expenditures for Negro pupils from $14 to $78 per annum.'[2]

Ernest W. Swanson and John A. Griffin, in their statistical survey, *Public Education in the South Today and Tomorrow*,

[1] Shoemaker and Others, *With All Deliberate Speed* (New York: Harper & Brothers, 1957), p. 93.

[2] Ginzberg and Bray, *The Uneducated* (New York: Columbia University Press, 1953), p. 193.

make the point that 'the out-migration of southern peoples means that the quality of public education in the South, especially that available to the Negro population, has more than academic importance for the nation as a whole and for certain selected non-southern states in particular'.[1] To this it might be added that the farm-to-city shift means that the quality of Southern rural education is of obvious concern to urban school systems, both South and North.

Now that Negroes are being dispersed from their original Southern rural habitat, the education the young get is important everywhere they go. The numbers of Negro children help make it important. 'In 1950 the number of children between the ages of five and seventeen equalled 30 per cent of the adults aged twenty to sixty-four in the population of the North East. In the South the ratio of children to adults of working age was 44 per cent. This difference reflects in the first instance differences in the birth rates of the two regions. The difference in birth rates in turn reflects the higher percentage of Negroes and rural population in the South. For instance, the ratio of children to urban white adults in the South is identical with the average for the North East—30. On the other hand, the Southern white farm population has a ratio of 56 per cent. Southern Negroes who live in urban centres show a slightly higher ratio than the Southern urban whites—40 compared to 30. But the really striking ratio is the one that indicates that among the Negro farm population of the South there are nine children for every ten adults! There can be no doubt that the burden of educating children is much heavier in the South, particularly the rural South, than in the heavily industrialized North East. The differences are so great that, although the continuing urbanization of the South and migration out of the South are doubtlessly narrowing the gap, it will long remain. One of the major products of the South is babies. One of its major exports to other parts of the country is young adults.'[2]

Negro children are attending school in greater numbers,

---

[1] Ernest W. Swanson and John A. Griffin, *Public Education in the South Today and Tomorrow* (Chapel Hill, N. C.: University of North Carolina Press, 1955).

[2] Ginzberg and Bray, *op. cit.*, pp. 188-89.

F*

starting at earlier ages and remaining in school longer so as to advance the level of education received. Negro parents and Negro youth themselves are conscious of the fact they must prepare for a future that is theirs, in a sense that the futures of other generations of Negroes have not been. This position makes them increasingly insistent that they secure the education they see themselves as needing, rather than accept an education another group may consider as being adequate for them.

About the matter of schooling, young Negroes have learned more from outside experiences than from class instruction during the past decade. As an institution around which controversy has centred, the public school has come up for reassessment. Negro children now know more about the provisions and operations of public schools than most adults did ten years ago. They have reasons for wanting the best possible education, not just having some schooling. This has been something in the last analysis they have had to do themselves. They had to go through hostile crowds and into classrooms where they were unwelcome. No parent or friend, or even advocate could do this for them. They did it for themselves in Clinton and Little Rock and Charlotte. When Negro teenagers made these pioneering journeys, with television following their progress for other Negro children everywhere to see, the Negro child got another kind of preparation for the future. These children are aware that others may make opportunities possible for them, but they alone can take advantage of an opportunity. They must be prepared for this as an unpleasant experience.

The Negro child in the South today has a better understanding of the Supreme Court, the Presidency, and the Congress than foregoing generations enjoyed, especially in an understanding that relates these institutions directly to his fortunes and welfare. Experiences of Negro youth in this decade and their discussion have provided an uncommon education in the value content of American culture, including political principles and processes of the government under which we live. Action and counter-action in regard to desegregation of schools, with a continuous reporting of these in the press and through radio and television, have provided an intimate review of democratic principles and democratic procedures in a context that has particular meaning for children and youth. Perhaps no other generation of young people has had so intensive an indoctrination in the American value system and certainly none has had the inconsistencies and contradictions so clearly presented to it. Southern children and youth have had conflicting social expectations defined for them and negations of these expectations spelled out in detail. No other generation of the young has been so confronted with the bright illusions of our political institutions or has had these illusions so ruthlessly attacked. Our political system has been the subject of continuing public debate during the decade, a debate marked by detraction, defiance, and challenge of institutions that previous generations had been taught to idealize and regard as sacrosanct. Since 1955, there has been court litigation over compliance with the Supreme Court's decision ordering desegregation of schools. Local plans and state legislation that would defy, evade, and delay compliance have been in court all over the South and on the first pages of the newspapers all this while.

Final decision has not been left to legislators, public officials, or the courts. People, banded together in organizations of various sorts of pressure and propaganda groups, have debated the status of Negro youth now and in the future. Most adhere to non-violent aims and methods. The championing organizations, particularly the NAACP, have been publicized and attributed power and influence far beyond their abilities, but in a degree that has certainly impressed the Negro child. Negro youth have learned how pressure groups are organized and the strategies and tactics they use. They are observing means that may be used to effect social and political actions, as well as techniques to prevent and obstruct these by an organized minority. How they will use these skills in social manipulation remains to be seen. Lessons in direct social action, in subversion, and in thwarting the popular will provide tools for use for ill as well as for good.

Negro youth have learned that some action for the common welfare must be taken by the federal government, and that those who argue most loudly for States' rights leave undone vitally important social tasks. They know how remiss local government can be in providing for public services, for security of the person and for enjoyment of citizenship rights. Their preparation for the future includes an expectation that the federal government can do and will do certain social tasks essential to the magnitude of their problems. The sit-ins, freedom rides and other direct action taken by young Negroes against segregation have been entered into with anticipation that public opinion outside of the South and protection by the federal government would support their efforts. A few of the youths were committed to 'non-violence' as a philosophy, more saw it as a tactical device, and others expected to force support from federal authority against the minorities of the Southern oligarchy.

The experience of Negro children in the South during the past decade might well be expected to have affected their conception of themselves as college students and young adults. Their behaviour and conduct offer evidence of some attributes of their self-image. Their self-esteem ranges from pride to bumptiousness. Ideas they hold about their opportunities are expressed by some in striving to realize an ambition, and by others in a demand for unearned rewards. Consciousness of having powerful and influential advocates of their greater opportunity is expressed in quiet confidence by some and in a challenging arrogance by others. Encouragement to venture where their parents did not dare has affected the respect shown for parents and teachers who urge caution and restraint. As in all revolutionary circumstances in which a new freedom is gained, there is considerable aimless, random, irresponsible behaviour on the part of those who have no constructive goals. Uncertainty and a sense of inadequacy are revealed in a truculence that challenges any imposed discipline.

The one clear feature of the new self-image of Negro youth, of whatever status, is a sense of security expressed by assuming positive and sometimes aggressive attitudes and postures. A Southern white man who recently returned to the South after eight years in other parts of the world said that the most startling change he noticed was that, 'Negroes look you straight in the eye now.' The newly-gained confidence that young Negroes have in themselves and the feeling of security in expressing their aspirations appear to be a disturbing fact of contemporary Southern life that many Southern white people are loath to face.

The cherished illusion of Southern whites that Negroes were 'satisfied' with their status and opportunities—'their place'—is being clung to, despite accumulation of a mass of evidence negating it. During the decade a governor of Mississippi was positively flabbergasted when a conference of Negro educators called by him with full assurance that they would support his programme for voluntary segregation refused to do so. Southern whites should give heed to signals such as that given in an Alabama courtroom by an illiterate Negro from the witness stand, who looked in the eyes of the Attorney General of the State and replied to his question with, 'Naw, man, naw!' That the Attorney General got the signal, however he may have interpreted it, was shown in his refusal to ask for a contempt of court citation of the witness on the ground that he did not 'want to make a martyr' of this man.

Charles S. Johnson wrote in the *New York Times Magazine* in September 1956 what was to become the valedictory to his long career of studying race relations. He said: 'The present-day Southern Negro does not share the belief of the Southern white that he is inferior as a human being, even though he may earn lower wages and have fewer years of schooling. . . . What is for white Southerners most difficult to understand, in these days, is the absence of both the belief in inferiority and the simulation of this belief. The Southern Negro viewpoint is more broadly national than regional. There are very few, if any, Southern Negroes who do not want full American citizenship, even though there are undoubtedly those who, if they had it, would make no better use of it than some of their white counterparts. In philosophy the Southern Negro identification is with the nation and not with the Southern region, which is, in spirit, separatist.'

Negro youth strive to give the impression of not feeling inferior even if the behaviour of some is clear evidence that they are over-compensating for such feeling. Unfortunately, a type of juvenile delinquency among Negro children and youth is appearing in the South. It is expressed in challenges to the traditional authority of whiteness and to that of Negro adults who occupy their positions through white authority.

A white professor, of unquestioned sympathy for the Negro's aspirations to equality, spoke at a Negro college where what he had to say certainly gave no offence. When he finished he found the hat he left on a seat had been filled with insulting notes. The Negro professor who was his host discussed the happening with him and came to the sorrowful conclusion: 'Your fathers sowed the wind; you must reap the whirlwind.' A truly great friend of the Negro in the civil rights struggle in the South had a disturbing experience as just an unrecognized white man. Walking along a street in the city where he lives, he met five Negro youths moving briskly abreast filling the sidewalk. He stepped off the walk and let them pass. He was troubled, he said, because he knew white children were served lectures on their superiority and defiance of change with their breakfasts and he realized from his experience that Negro children were being taught something obverse to that. Thoughts of clashes between the young who were getting these contradictory indoctrinations saddened him.

Perhaps the most unfortunate aspect of the young Negro's conception of himself is that he must depend upon himself to carry his battle, with the support of few, if any, white people in his local community. Those whites who are sympathetic to his cause are silent for very good reasons of their own. Those who most loudly declare their 'friendship' for him are those who do so confidently asserting they know no 'good' Negro has aspirations of equality, and who denounce his heroes and threaten mayhem if he persists in pursuit of his ambitions. A state official in high office expressed this often repeated opinion: 'I'm the best friend the Negro ever had but integration will come only over my dead body.' If these are his white friends, he is convinced he has none. It is certainly unfortunate when Negro youth get the idea that they must 'protect themselves' or be prepared to do so because the duly constituted authority for preserving the security of citizens in their home communities leaves them at the mercy of enemies who would do violence to them.

Negro students have formed allies among white students all over the United States, and most significantly in Southern colleges and universities. Southern white students have participated in sit-ins, stand-ins, and freedom rides against formidable deterrents used by college and university officials. When hoodlums have violently attacked student non-violent demonstrations, the white demonstrators have been subjected to the most violent manhandling. Within white college communities, students who support continued segregation make miserable the lives of students who openly oppose it.

White college and university officials are subjected to the strongest pressure from the oligarchy and it is the rare official who resists continuing pressure. Officials of a college in Montgomery, Alabama, contrary to the policy stand taken by the Methodist Church that supports it, forbade students to attend interracial meetings, threatened them with expulsion and argued that they should withdraw from the institution. A Florida institution regulation, that students convicted of a crime would be dismissed, was used when white students who joined Negro students in violating a segregation ordinance were convicted in court. Trustees of white educational institutions who are members in good standing of the oligarchy have been unyielding in their pressure on college administrations to uphold the spirit of segregation and discrimination.

Several conferences of Southern white and Negro students have been sponsored by the Highlander Folk School at Monteagle, Tennessee, to which white students attending Northern colleges have come to meet with Negro students. One of these 'workshops' produced a report that was edited by a student committee from The University of the South and published under the title, *The Role of the Southern White Student in the Struggle for Social Justice*. The Highlander Folk School is perhaps the only institution in the South where Negro and white students can meet and discuss freely their common concerns.

Another feature of the new self-image is that young Negroes are seeing themselves as leaders, rather than as being in preparation for leadership. Students who suffer indignities as the first ones to enter desegregated schools with the responsibility for persisting in their attendance despite discouraging experiences feel this way. Students who challenged bus segregation in Tallahassee, those who staged a boycott in Orangeburg, and those who mounted a campaign to desegregate soft-drink establishments in Oklahoma had some of the feeling. The problem growing out of such a self-conception is the danger of intemperate actions that may draw reprisals in kind.

A third feature of the new self-image is that young Negroes do not feel themselves to be a helpless minority. Instead they consider the die-hard segregationists, whatever their positions may be in the community or however important may be the political offices they hold, to be the minority. And they scoff at them as ludicrous buffoons, clinging desperately to a lost cause. The young Negro in the South sees himself as belonging to the majority that includes the federal government, Negroes who have advanced outside the South, and white people of powerful influence outside the South. Problems posed by this feature of the new self-image are: 1. Raising an obstruction to an early rapprochement with young Southern whites, and 2. The possible disenchantment with their allies if they give too little or too tardy support.

A fourth feature of the new self-image is the belief that they hold to the great human values uncompromisingly. This is especially true in relating their struggle to the independence struggles of Asia and Africa. A problem raised by this conception is the possibility of joining the divisive black nationalist movements in the United States which would be a rejection of all the arduous struggle for integration with results of further tension and conflict.

The major issue the Negro youth's new image raises is what positive approaches may be taken for constructive productive humanists to mature out of the current personality conflicts in a setting of social confusion. Among the Negro youths who have taken leadership roles in sit-ins, stand-ins and freedom rides there are those who obviously have emotional problems. Some of them cannot be satisfied with a single victory but look for other battles to wage. There are those who have abandoned their college training and have given up career aspirations. Some show an insatiable hunger for recognition and public attention that can be satisfied only by role-playing crisis situations. So long as the Southern oligarchy makes crises possible there will be young Negroes playing roles in them which are now fully fashioned and stylized.

CHAPTER XII

Dangers Present and Not So Present

THE Southern oligarchy has given clear warning that disturbance of the order it has imposed and maintained is fraught with manifold dangers. These dangers, it warns, are immediate and present. The oligarchy can give these warnings with conviction and authority because the dangers are within themselves, or within circumstances they have created and which they control. They have provided the nation with object lessons on clear and present danger; the nation can but hold them responsible for their works.

Within the domain ruled by the oligarchy those who would disturb its peace by threatening changes in its order of things are warned to expect no security. Neither state governments nor local governments accept responsibility for safeguarding the lives or economic security of individuals who set upon a course contrary to the expressed wishes of the oligarchy. These malefactors of reckless temerity place in jeopardy their livelihood, limb, life, and peace of mind. The sacrifice of these rights must be accepted as calculated risks by those who would pioneer in bringing changes to the South. The circumstances, and the necessary action in these circumstances, produce the kind of milieu in which martyrdom occurs. Already martyrs have been made to the cause of full citizenship for Negroes. Lives already taken give warning that the lives of others will be required and serve notice that their taking under the rule of the oligarchy may be interpreted as a patriotic service. The unavenged dead bear eloquent testimony to this: Reverend Lee and Lamar Smith in Mississippi, and Mr and Mrs Harry Moore in Florida.

Americans who oppose violence, and those who feel revulsion in the wanton taking of human life, can only mourn with Negroes their martyrs. From the lips of the oligarchy we are warned to prepare for the likelihood of more martyrs being made. The already unpunished murderers invite to their ranks those who would be heroes of the cause of the oligarchy. There is the excellent prospect that those who fall armed with a ballot, or for a scarcely legible signature on a petition, or for the expression of a sentiment that the oligarchy does not appreciate hearing again will recruit, within and outside the South, men of all conditions to the ranks of those who mourn. Among the sorrowing, there will be some sensitive in the oligarchy who, after the manner of things in our time, have come to place and prestige along the only avenue by which these might be reached.

Robert J. Donovan in his book, *Eisenhower—The Inside Story*, cites J. Edgar Hoover as the source of a report to the President's Cabinet that, in an area checked by the FBI, there was a 400 per cent increase in the shipment of firearms. It is obvious that some white people are not content to accept decisions made by the courts. It is obvious that there are some Negroes who are prepared to reply to violence with violence. Equally obvious is the fact that local law enforcement officials are not vigilant in preventing a mass arming. Obviously, the oligarchy does not see shooting battles as a sequence to legal and verbal battles as unfortunate occurrences.

There is a very good likelihood that many will suffer anguish of one sort or another. Negro leaders, little known beyond the communities in which they live, have known the fear of threats and whether they can be delivered or not. The Negro leader, in a small city, who has removed all trees and shrubbery from the grounds about his home and has placed floodlights, so that all approaches to his house are well illuminated, is hardly a unique case. Other men too will toss sleepless or turn in troubled sleep because of threats made against them. An aged mother has repeatedly answered her telephone in the small hours of the morning to be told where to go to find the body of her son who had challenged the ways of the oligarchy. Other mothers will know troubled spirits due to the fear that one of these muffled messages may prove to be accurate.

There are those terrorists in the South who disavow violence but feel no compunction about joining in actions so long as they may be construed to be *legal*. The restraint they show in keeping within the bounds of legality is held to be virtue of a commendable order. These decry the weapon-wielding men of violence, while proclaiming themselves to be patriots of a zeal greater than the violent. Their deeds for the sacred cause show greater valour because they are worked in wisdom rather than in passion.

These exponents of legalistic zeal disparage those who go beyond propriety and seek to conceal their identities by mask or by acting under cover of darkness. These take pride in unmasked sadism as they act in their ordinary influential capacities in the community—a banker curtly denying a Negro farmer a production loan; a wholesale jobber refusing a Negro storekeeper merchandise; an employer dismissing a long-time employee; or a local government official making new laws, or interpreting anew old laws.

Few in the oligarchy can disavow those organized in the White Citizens Councils, the Southern Gentlemen, the Federation for Constitutional Government, and others, all of which are committed to preserve segregation at all costs short of violence. All of the prestige the oligarchy can summon is lent to the works of these groups, as by Senator J. Strom Thurmond of South Carolina:

'It would be submission to cowardice if we failed to use every lawful means to protect the rights of the people. We are free morally and legally to oppose the (Supreme Court) decision. We must fight to the end.'

From the *Southern School News*, the source from which Senator Thurmond is quoted, some other reports of the stands taken by gentlemen of the oligarchy:

'At a pro-segregation rally in Memphis, Curt Copeland of Little Rock, Ark.: Southern preachers "are so carried away with this brotherhood mess of trash they haven't got the guts to preach the doctrine of segregation which is the doctrine of God".'

'State Education Commissioner Quill Cope, speaking to super-intendents at the Tennessee Education Association's 88th annual convention: "All of you know the problem we are facing in our schools. I plead with each of you to keep emotionalism out of this matter as far as possible. We have more than 100 local school systems in Tennessee and I don't presume to tell any one of them how to meet this problem. I urge you to consult with your local leaders on it."'

'Candidates for political office in Alabama were sent the following questionnaires?

1. Will you give your wholehearted support to the action which has already been taken by the legislature of Alabama toward maintaining segregation?
2. Are you willing to advise those voters, Negro or others who favour the policy of integration, that they may not only expect no support for their policies from you, but also that they may expect you to fight with every means at your disposal any attempt to bring integration to this state?
3. Has the NAACP or any other organization dedicated to the breakdown of Alabama policies of segregation made any financial contribution directly or indirectly to your campaign?
4. Do you here and now deny the Negro Vote?
5. Do you here and now say to the Negro that you do not want his vote?
6. Are you willing to submit to this office a notarized list of organizations contributing to your campaign?
7. Do you believe in the Citizens Councils of Alabama Movement?
8. Are you a member of a unit of the Citizens Councils of Alabama?
9. If no, will you join a unit of the Citizens Councils of Alabama?'

These are not the sentiments of those who practice violence or those who advocate gradualism. They are open threats to all that the Citizens Councils are prepared to claim the political scalps of those who disagree with them. Such efforts by the Citizens Councils to nullify the growing Negro vote amounts to a form of psychological terrorism.

There is the real and present danger of the deterioration of relationships between Negro and white people in local communities. Tensions and ill-will may be expected to increase for a period of time. Many people within the South and outside of it will deplore the 'worsening of race relations'. Editor C. A. McKnight of the *Charlotte Observer* commented:

'It can be said as a fact that race relations in many parts of the region (the South) are at the lowest ebb in a generation. In my opinion, what is desperately needed now is a "breathing spell" during which emotions may subside and some of the misunderstanding be cleared up.'

Those who regret the racial tensions now existing fail to take into account the simple facts about them. The prevailing discord is not based on misunderstanding, but on a full understanding between the contending forces for and against segregation.

There was peace of a sort and racial co-operation in the communities of the South, but it was a peace dependent on the Negro's accepting a subordinate position in the society. The oligarchy has repeated time and again its terms for peace to be the acceptance of this subordination by Negroes and their renunciation of the challenges made to that subordination.

Those who plead with the Negro leadership to accept peace by giving the oligarchy a breathing spell to adjust itself to the gains which Negroes have made *in principle*, without doubt make the plea in good faith. They do not seem to realize that they are asking Negroes to continue patiently in the role of subordination. For Negroes this appears to be too great a price to pay for peace. The greater danger to them seems to lie, not in the calculated risks and the apparently inevitable sacrifices Negroes must make to have the principles they have won translated into practice, but in their failure to press for this translation into practice.

The dangers in the failure of Negroes to press for their legal due are several. There is the danger in giving the oligarchy confidence in threat and intimidation as being useful in flouting what is legal. This is a danger to both Negroes and to the South. Negroes must not give any assurance that violence or terroristic means 'short of violence' are effective weapons to be held in readiness for future use. No danger now appears so great as this truce, at the behest of those friendly to the Negro, which would be interpreted as a victory by the oligarchy. The oligarchy would have won a capitulation proving the efficacy of their being un-compromising.

Men of professed friendliness have long asked patience of the Negro. They have seen the South do nothing about giving the Negro the vote until outside pressure was put on the oli-garchy to do so. They have seen the oligarchy refuse to take seriously giving Negroes school terms of equal length to those of whites, and the salaries of Negro teachers kept to a fraction of those white teachers received. These things changed not at all until the law and public opinion from outside of the South were used. The great danger to race relations is in the Negroes' loss of faith in their supposed friends. There is no danger so great (in accepting or reciprocating enmity) as that coming from disillusionment with friends in time of crisis.

In truth, behind the heat and light of the political controversy there is an immense hard, cold, economic problem that begs attention. Should there be a truce in the integration struggle, and should the shouting suddenly die away, the community, the state, and the nation would have this problem looming over them. Still there would be migration of Negroes in search of jobs. Still there would be Negroes engaged in trade and in the pro-fessions in the South who faced problems due to the reduction in the clientele that would be expected to support them. The bankers, merchants, and politicians in the South know this. Behind the screen of the integration furore they can go about the pruning of the South's economy by removing undergrowth and lopping off less productive twigs and branches. What they find extraneous they can cast out or scare away to other parts of the country. That their long-used and now cast-off Negro minority should prove troublesome to other parts of the nation gives them sardonic satisfaction.

Prospects appear dim for the solution of the problems of the black ghettos in northern industrial cities. The persistence may be attributed to the continuous migration, which means there are always first generation migrants with all of the handicaps that limit such a first generation. The progress of second and third generations is obscured by the maladjustment of the first generation. Opportunities for the employment of new-comers possessing agricultural and domestic-service skills are limited, and competition for these jobs may be expected to be keen. Low-paid jobs such as these place people at an income level that can provide only substandard living conditions.

Northern industrial cities need to be prepared for no relief from the problems of migrants. There is the danger that the problem will become greater. Provision of housing and re-training of migrants for productive usefulness may require a greater financial outlay and more imagination than has hitherto been called for. Frank assessment and planning might be undertaken to rehabilitate and adjust these people to urban industrial life. There is the danger of these migrants having directed at them resentment for their shortcomings and disabilities, rather than having it directed at the matrix in which these disabilities were conceived and nurtured.

Unemployment and underemployment within the South are dangers that need to be considered. Here again, there is the problem of re-training to equip people with skills to replace those that have become obsolete. Machine-operation and machine-maintenance skills will be needed for those who are to be employed in either industry or mechanized agriculture. There is the danger of the masses of Negroes in the South continuing in a submerged economic position as that position becomes even more of a disadvantaged one. As new machines make dirty and burdensome tasks fewer, the stigma attached to such jobs will disappear. With the disappearance of the stigma will go the 'Negro job'. Negroes will be in competition with white workers for these jobs. The present apprenticeship and training programmes put the Negro in a position of disadvantage in this competition.

Already signals are being flashed in sombre warning. Negroes are not being employed in new industries in the South in the proportion they are of the labour force. This problem is not merely the Negro's problem; it is as much the South's problem.

The economic health of the region cannot be advanced so long as there is a large part of the population lacking skills, and limited as to employment opportunities. The whole economy will be affected by a large group of low-earning power and a consequent low-purchasing power.

Industries moving into many places in the South are making efforts to remove distinctions according to race in the employment and upgrading of workers. These industries can exercise some control over their employees and hire them under terms that commit them to work in harmony with other workers, regardless of race. The labour organizations can use the controls they have to commit their members to co-operation on the job in a like manner. Both management and labour find themselves annoyed and know some frustration in the laws of the oligarchy, which make difficult the working out of this problem. Requirement of separate facilities for Negro and white workers are costly and inconvenient. Nor are all-Negro or all-white forces in plants a solution. Feelings of antagonism developed in the exclusion of one race or the other stir resentment that may have far-reaching results.

Fair employment laws are bitterly opposed by those in power who have legislated conditions of unfair employment, by denying employers the freedom to employ unhampered and by denying workers the freedom to work unhampered. In one Southern city an industrial plant that hired many Negroes acquired a new plant site and prepared to expand its facilities, when the city council re-zoned the area forbidding plant construction there. The large number of Negro employees was admitted to be a factor in the re-zoning, which made it necessary for the company to find and purchase another plant site. The oligarchy finds divers ways to stultify the economy it claims it would develop.

The significance of fully employed and well-paid Negro workers in the South is summed up in a message sent to a convention of Southern planters at Vicksburg in 1879—'The sands may fly but the earth remains'. These planters were concerned about the migration to Kansas at that time. Migration from the South may be expected to continue and to be accelerated, but the majority of the Negro population will remain in the

South for a long time to come. The South must face up to having this productive population or know the disadvantages of a population that suffers from limited earnings and an economy suffering from limited spending.

The problem is not purely economic, but is affected by the constraints put on the economy by the government. How the oligarchy operates to preserve a condition of disadvantage may be illustrated by the policy in regard to defence training during World War II. Defence training classes had been established for some time in a community, with only one class for Negroes. This was a class of thirteen being trained to be blacksmiths. A committee of Negroes waited on the superintendent of schools. He explained that it was a matter that would have to be presented to the board of education. However, he warned the committee that the board of education would not look favourably on providing classes they requested because the employers would not hire Negroes given such training, the United States Employment Service would not certify Negroes for such jobs, and that the labour unions would not approve of Negroes being given the training. In the interim between the interview with the superintendent and meeting with the board of education, the committee secured statements from employers saying that they would hire Negroes so trained, a statement from the USES saying that they would be certified, and succeeded in having the Central Trades Council of the American Federation of Labour pass a resolution requesting the board of education to provide such classes. The Chairman of the board of education did not promise to provide the classes. Instead he made a speech saying the problem was one of getting the Office of War Manpower to provide funds. This occurred in one of the southern cities where there was politeness, rather than the frequent terse refusal that some boards of education give to such requests.

The danger in some areas of activity lies in the ability of the oligarchy to shift responsibility from itself, in the exercise of its obvious powers, to groups whose sentiments it claims to respect. These groups are difficult to arraign in terms of their policies. So far as the laws are concerned the oligarchy makes those and enforces them. It is a convenient stratagem to justify its laws and the manner in which they are enforced in terms of an amorphous public opinion that binds it to the course of action that it follows.

Negroes themselves present a danger in that the disabilities developed and preserved over generations will not be removed immediately. Those disabilities with which Negro adults are now encumbered must be reckoned with. Economic insecurity and occupational limitation will move many to seek what security they can find in the places where they live. This acceptance of disadvantaged status for themselves is associated with the aspirations they have for their children. The parents have a feeling that they must get along as best they can in order to give to their children opportunities which they themselves did not know. This ambivalence in sentiments is a confusing one to many people. The Negro parent who is apparently adjusted to subservience and accepts the prevailing order is the despair of those who would move quickly in bringing about change. These parents are aware of their limitations and have a real concern about securing the means necessary to advance their children beyond the condition to which they are inured. The danger this state of mind represents is its becoming more desperate and showing itself in a more complete obeisance, felt to be necessary to give their children opportunity.

A spirit of laissez faire on the part of private industry and educational foundations may serve to retard the advancement of the opportunities. Private industry can exert pressure on local governments. This is particularly true in the South, where inducements are being offered to secure the location of industries. When industry accepts the largesse of the oligarchy, and pays for it by subscribing to the dictates of the oligarchy, it initiates a chain of circumstances from which it may find it difficult to extricate itself later. The oligarchy is not above applying pressure in the form of boycotts against the very industries it has urged to locate plants in the South. Negroes are learning the usefulness of the boycott as a weapon. The industry is faced with the decision as to whether it will respect law or the 'laws' of the oligarchy.

Sources of funds for educational purposes are of tremendous importance to the maintenance of the private colleges and universities. These institutions remain the great hope for the training of leadership and an elite in the South. In times past the foundations have on occasion defined the course of realism to be that of cooperating with the oligarchy on its terms. This course of action as it reflected confidence in the good faith of the oligarchy proved to be unrealistic.

The Julius Rosenwald Fund during its existence did proceed to use its funds to secure the commitment of public funds to Negro education. The 5,000 school buildings it succeeded in getting constructed required investment by the local communities. At the conclusion of this programme of school construction, the Rosenwald Fund revealed that it had borne 18 per cent of the construction costs. Arrangements were negotiated by which new teachers' colleges in Mississippi and Georgia were provided for Negroes. On the sheer evidence of need, all funds invested in Negro education in the South may be justified. The philanthropy that went to Negro state colleges was too often accepted as relieving the states themselves of responsibility for these institutions. The private colleges, which provided instruction of a higher order than that made available in the state-supported institutions, were constantly in disfavour with the state educational authorities because of the instruction they did provide. Some of them taught Latin instead of mattress-making. These institutions, in the future as in the past, may be expected to provide a superior quality of instruction. They will continue to be dependent on private philanthropy for support. Compromise between the foundations and the oligarchy is a danger since it constitutes a threat to the support of the best education that some Negroes will receive for some years yet to come. Another danger in this connection is that of the reluctant or misguided donor, reaching the conclusion that integration is here and that the best course is to support the white institutions that have a policy of integration. Funds to these in endorsement of their policies are well spent but the need for the Negro private college did not disappear on May 17, 1954.

There is some danger in the success of the oligarchy labelling those who espouse the citizenship rights of Negroes as 'Communists'. Members of the oligarchy are in a similar situation to that of the woman who defended her son, who was serving a sentence in the penitentiary, by declaring, 'He's in the penitentiary but he ain't there for no communism.' Any sin but communism is excusable in this kind of thinking.

There is danger in the oligarchy calling the signals for its police force to attack praying and singing Negroes. Encouragement of white mobs to gather and threaten the non-violent by jailing the latter for 'disturbing the peace' or 'incitement to riot', while taking no action to disperse the mob has already borne its bitter fruit. Representatives of the oligarchy who persecute the NAACP and vilify Reverend Martin Luther King, Jr. and his organization, the Southern Christian Leadership Conference, have already brought into being the 'Black Muslims' who reject Christianity, advocate violence against white people, disclaim the identification 'Negro', and heap scorn upon all Negro organizations and their leadership. The Black Muslims are a negation of the philosophy of integration; they reject the large history of legal action by Negro organizations to be 'just Americans'. Every official of the federal government since 1876 and every spokesman for the Christian religion has responsibility for permitting the rebellious oligarchy to produce this group and any mischief it may make. Negro leadership may not be absolved from its share of this responsibility since each of its compromises with the oligarchy made the appearance of such a group more certain.

These represent clear and present dangers in the unsettled conditions that exist today. A new adjustment may be anticipated with confidence, but prior to this adjustment these dangers must be met and countered so as to further the common welfare of the Negro, the South, and the Nation.

Not so present are those dangers about which the orators of the oligarchy wax vehement. The favourite danger seen by the oligarchy is intermarriage and a consequent 'mongrelization'. There are those who see the only solution of the race problem in the United States to be in the disappearance of the Negro as an identifiable group. This process of assimilation is what the oligarchy describes as the mongrelization of the population. The oligarchy in its diatribes on the subject cannot fail to imbue such a union with fascination. It seems strange for the oligarchy to admit that, after all of these generations in which its spokesmen have harangued on the subject, it remains necessary to prohibit

intermarriage by law and deter it by use of violence. They are
admitting that they have not succeeded in instilling fear in
Negroes and that they have failed to make the Negro mate
unattractive to whites. From the record it appears that the
danger of extensive intermarriage is not immediate. This is by
no means to say that one should not be free to take to bed and
board any partner fancy may dictate.

For the oligarchy the second great danger is Negro political
domination. When Negroes vote, Negroes will hold political
office. However, racism does not appear to be so strong as to
permit a prediction of political cleavage along racial lines. The
removal of racial barriers seems to remove such cleavage. The
oligarchy, in its pronouncements, admits failure in this too. Despite all of the efforts of the oligarchy they have not succeeded
in developing strong hatreds between whites and Negroes. There
is ample evidence that, when Negroes and whites are free to
organize and to act as they choose politically, there are whites
and Negroes on either side of any division. It would be ironic
if, in this current struggle, the efforts of the oligarchy should
have an unfortunate success. As a matter of fact there appears
to be little danger to the political careers of the talented members of the oligarchy. Their political lives cannot be said to be
at stake in so far as threats from Negroes are concerned. Those
of the oligarchy who are blatant racists, and who have compounded insult with injury, know full well that their political
fortunes depend upon the success of their current campaign to
preserve the oligarchy regardless of what it costs the United
States.

The National Association for the Advancement of Coloured
People represents a clear and present danger to the oligarchy.
No danger the oligarchy has met has proved to be so consistently exasperating. No greater embarrassment could be visited
on the oligarchy than forcing it to give an accounting of its use
of its public trust in the courts of justice in the full glare of
public opinion. There the lawyers of the NAACP have asked only
that which the judges could not deny—justice as written in the
law of the United States. Unable to match the simple dignity of
the NAACP attorneys in their pleadings, unable to make defens-
ible legal cases for their abuse of their public trusts, the oli-

garchy has been goaded into the declaration of its own outlawry. None should be surprised that the NAACP has earned
the hatred of the oligarchy. Hardly a worse humiliation for the
oligarchy can be imagined than to come into court where they
could not match the legal arguments of Negro lawyers. Members
of the oligarchy who have long worked their will without giving
account for their acts find themselves polite if discomfited in
the dock under oath declaring themselves culpable. School
superintendents, college presidents, election officials—all members of the oligarchy in good standing have left courtrooms—
proved to be men of questionable honour. Behind them hapless
lawyers of all sorts, city attorneys, attorneys general of states,
who could not win their cases failed even to save face for them.
The ultimatum given by the NAACP is one that all Americans
should in honour share: respect the laws of the United States
or wear the indignity of outlawry.

It is saddening to find other Americans who join the oligarchy
in damning the NAACP. One is at a complete loss to understand
how these men can, in honesty, bracket together the NAACP and
the White Citizens Councils as both being extremists. It is hard
to believe these men can, in good conscience, give comfort to the
oligarchy by justifying their past sins and present outlawry
on the grounds that the NAACP forced them to this behaviour.
It is rather like saying that an incorruptible policeman makes
thieves of thieves. To behold these men of character joining
the assault on the NAACP is one of the most discouraging
spectacles witnessed since May 17, 1954. Guiltless of any
violation of federal law, the NAACP has been persecuted under
the 'laws' of Alabama, Georgia, Louisiana, Texas and in South
Carolina.

Those who have determined to destroy the NAACP, because it
has been successful in open forthright legal action, belong to or
give comfort to the White Citizens Councils. This organization
makes no secret of its mission as being that of contravening
federal, and sometimes state, law. Even among the oligarchy
there are those who have seen the danger in a group that advocates disrespect of law, in contrast to the NAACP's invoking of
the law. Tolerance of any group that advocates subversion, sedition, and anarchy and acts outside of lawful procedures is an

obvious danger. Fifty such organizations, that count among their members Southern governors, legislators and men of influence and prestige, as well as their deluded supporters, have operated since World War II in the South. The great danger to the United States is their fascistic influence.

CHAPTER XIII

Consent of the Governed

THE ROLE of the Southern oligarchy in maintaining a *status quo* in which its position of power and the Negro's position of subordination remain unaltered has been described in some detail. Attention has not been focused upon group sentiments, personal antipathies, or prejudices of any sort because these are not the directive forces in the situation. Law and the application of law are directive. Whether these sentiments, antipathies, and prejudices exist or not is beside the point. The laws and their enforcement are vested in a group that makes a bold claim to the power of government. The crux of the question is the use of this power and the expressed intent of those having power to preserve a political order without regard for the sentiments and feelings of some, if not most, of the people they rule.

The crucial issue in democratic government is the vote: how many citizens cast ballots and how these ballots are cast. All political regimes except the oligarchy regard government based on the affirmative consent of the governed as being of utmost importance. One-party totalitarian governments make a point of securing approval of the regime by ballots of the eligible electorate even when there is no alternative choice. Peoples who are denied a choice under unpopular governments make one by abstaining from elections. The Southern oligarchy is an uncommon political phenomenon in its anxiety to restrict the electorate.

All adversaries of the oligarchy are concerned about vote restrictions within its hegemony. The most conservative opponents seek the two-party system in the South, even if this means Tweedledee vs. Tweedledum, as in Texas, where a conservative

Republican was elected to fill the Senate seat of Vice President Lyndon Johnson in 1961. At various historical periods new parties have attempted to destroy the one-party system, only to know defeat by a political organization that controlled the complete election machinery.

The Kennedy administration, mindful of the lessons taught Franklin D. Roosevelt by the oligarchy, has shown its intent to provide free elections in the South by use of its powers to make it possible for all eligible citizens to register and vote. This means that President Kennedy has no illusions about securing the necessary legislation for a liberal programme so long as the reactionary representatives of the oligarchy have parliamentary powers.

It is highly doubtful that given a choice the people of South Carolina age twenty-one years and older would have the benighted J. Strom Thurmond of South Carolina in the Senate of the United States in 1961 to ask the Senate for $75,000 to 'investigate' the influence of Senator J. William Fulbright, an enlightened member of the oligarchy, who is Chairman of the Senate Foreign Relations Committee, for asking that officers of the Army of the United States be restrained from political indoctrination of men under their command. Be it remembered that this J. Strom Thurmond assumed the chieftainship of the Southern Rebels as presidential candidate on the States' rights ticket in 1948.

All over the South in cities and towns there have been organized voter leagues, which have banded together in state organizations to increase the electorate. Through many convenient devices they have been stymied in getting people on registration rolls and getting those once registered to cast ballots.

There remains the question of the sensible use of the ballots by those so long denied it. The new mood is against the party boss pattern with its 'drink-of-whisky and fish-sandwich' voters. They are the simple people, who respond to the blandishments of politicians who entertain them and ask their votes even against their own best interest.

Highlander Folk School, on the Cumberland Plateau in Tennessee, devised and successfully used a programme of citizenship education. In an experimental period it demonstrated that in three months an illiterate Negro adult could be taught to read and write, and to understand the voting requirements if the latter were used as subject matter. Its programme was expanded to other parts of the South and for some classes twenty-five out of thirty students secured their voter registrations in three months. The oligarchy promptly moved in on Highlander Folk School to close it up. However, the adult education principle had been demonstrated as effective. Citizenship schools are now being conducted over the South by Reverend Martin Luther King's Southern Christian Leadership Conference, the American Missionary Association and other groups. Myles Horton, the sad-eyed Southern white man who started the school as a young man twenty-eight years ago says, ' the programme is important, I give all our experience to any group that will use it, I encourage the staff we have trained to work with any organization that will make more people intelligent voters '. There are reservations like the one expressed by Professor Morris Mitchell of Putney Graduate School who says, ' If Negroes who clamour for first-class citizenship behave as stupidly as other "first class" citizens in America I don't think it is worth it.'

There is no way of knowing how great a number of the people under the rule of the oligarchy are in agreement with its practices and policies, since they are not given the opportunity to express their views. The organized protests by the oligarchy in those places where desegregation is threatened involve a noticeable minority of the people who live in the community. Where desegregation has occurred, the antagonism to it has not received support of a general public opposition. There is strong indication that those in disagreement with the oligarchy are many and that those who are uncommitted or indifferent are more numerous.

There may be a problem of the education, the indoctrination, the conversion of great groups of people involved in successfully making a shift from segregation to integration. The discussion given here does not deal with that problem. Rather, it concerns itself with the political problem, one that has to do with those who have power using it to exact conformity with their views by fear and force, when unsure that public opinion will support their policies.

The employment of fear and force appears anachronistic in this age, when the engineering of consent has become a specialized skill with refined mechanisms developed for thought control and opinion formation. Public relations artists have so developed their skills as to undertake, with confidence and sometimes with insolence, to package and sell ideas as well as toilet soap. The efficient use of these skills and techniques has brought into our vocabularies the concept 'brain-washing', when used by those who oppose us. Members of the Supreme Court of the United States have been accused by members of the oligarchy as having undergone a brain-washing. When used to convince people to the views we advocate, the practices are considered to be praiseworthy, if interpreted as *defining* and *clarifying* for the confused or giving voice to the inarticulate.

Clumsy and camouflaged command of consent through fear and force is outmoded and in disrepute. This barbaric survival that the Southern oligarchy would preserve for its use, at best, secures only unstable consent and is always threatened with revolt. Countering the oligarchy calls for the rejection of the use of fear and force by an elite insistent upon wielding power. This is not to suggest that thoughtful people should accept as replacement for these the cynical manipulation of opinion by engineers of consent. No endorsement is intended for popular public relations devices used to 'sell' everything, from a deodorant cream, to the United Nations. Rather, it is to indicate that among devices for engineering consent, fear and force have no respectable standing.

What has been referred to throughout this discussion as the conflict between the oligarchy and the Negro is much more than that. In terms of ultimates it resolves itself into a question of the rightness of government resting on the freely given consent of the governed, or government by an elite that commands consent through fear and force. Looked at from this perspective, what is commonly regarded as the 'Negro's struggle' is one that would confirm or reject a basic democratic principle. This principle is one that few in America would deny as an article of their political faith, however remiss they should be in its practice. Even the oligarchy mouths it as an article of faith while exerting every effort to negate it in practice. The struggle becomes a crusade for re-dedication to the American faith, un-expurgated, and its validation in general practice.

The Negroes, in their long struggle for government based on the consent of the governed, have at all times expressed faith that democracy in America is sufficiently virile to contain and neutralize the oligarchy. Their insistence has been on having the opportunity to live under a government that is representative of them. They have continued to dramatize the disadvantage of those who are denied representation in government. They symbolize all to whom representation is denied and all whose consent is commanded through force and fear. They have left no doubt about the importance of democratic processes being essential to the application of democratic principles.

Editor William O. Walker in his column, 'Down the Big Road', for the July 1, 1961 issue of his paper the *Cleveland Call Post* quotes Edward R. Murrow, director of the United States Information Agency:

> 'Assessed in terms of their impact on the American image abroad, the violence against the "Freedom Riders" in Alabama, and to a lesser extent their jailing in Mississippi, have had a harmful effect.'

Yet, there are good northern white Americans on John F. Kennedy's team who feel some blood brothership with the members of the oligarchy. They would keep democracy from America another hundred years because they sympathize with their 'kind'.

Any elite that usurps the rights of the people and that abrogates the power of the people to itself is destructive to democracy. The aspirations of any elite to do these things represent a threat to our form of government and our way of life. Safeguarding the mechanisms for expression of consent has been demonstrated to be the very foundation upon which democracy rests.

The approach Negroes have made to the problem of an ambitious elite has been an essentially healthy one. They have refrained from expressing desire for vengeance, retribution, or reprisals. They suggest no punitive measures against the oligarchy. They promise no extension of devisiveness based on rancour.

The oligarchy can offer no evidence of threat to its democratic rights and privileges upon relinquishing its position as an elite. It stands to lose only the role of elite. That role itself is something that no group in a democratic society has any justification for expecting.

That eternal vigilance, on which the survival of a democracy depends, requires the recognition of the inevitable elites when they appear. The influence that these elites succeed in exerting becomes a test of the support an elite can claim when it bids to usurp the rights and to arrogate to itself the powers that belong to the people. Acceptance of it as a dissident minority and tolerance for its dissidence are the fullest possible acknowledgement of the strength of the democracy. To contain and neutralize the efforts of the elite precludes its becoming a threat to the integrity of the democratic system. The acknowledgement of dissidence and treatment of it with respect becomes a safeguard against subversion.

Violence or pressures that violate the spirit of democracy, when employed by the dissidents, give evidence that they have grown desperate from being frustrated by their inability to subvert. Strict adherence to the prescribed uses of the police power and the judicial power denies sympathy for dissidence or the martyring of the dissidents. When the prescribed uses of the police power and the judicial power are set aside, and special legislation or violence or pressures contrary to the democratic spirit are used, the health of the democracy is suspected of having reached a precarious state. The invoking of these special measures calls for a re-examination of the power structure in the society.

The consent of the governed in a democracy should not be construed either as the abdication of the powers of the electorate when it delegates authority, or as the surrender of decision-making to an elite. Neither does it mean that the authority delegated to elected representative includes license to exceed the prescribed powers that are inherent in the office.

The Southern oligarchy has assumed the role of a power elite. It has used its power to usurp the rights and arrogate to itself the powers of the people. It has commanded the consent of the governed through force and fear. It has expressed a dissidence directed against cohesion in the nation.

In their struggle, Negroes represent those Americans who are committed to cohesion and oppose division. They believe that this should be One Nation Indivisible—Under God, and Under Law. They lay claim to the support of Americans who share this article of faith and see it to depend in practice on the expressed consent of the governed. So long as an oligarchy rules anywhere, there is government without the freely-given consent of the governed.

WITHDRAWAL